TALK TO THE SNAIL

TALK
TO THE
SNAIL

Ten Commandments for
Understanding the French

STEPHEN CLARKE

BLOOMSBURY

Published by Bloomsbury USA, New York
Distributed to the trade by Holtzbrinck Publishers

All papers used by Bloomsbury USA are natural, recyclable products made from wood grown in well-managed forests. The manufacturing processes conform to the environmental regulations of the country of origin.

Library of Congress Cataloging-in-Publication Data has been applied for.

ISBN 1-59691-309-6
ISBN-13 978-1-59691-309-7

First published in the United Kingdom by Bantam Press in 2006
First U.S. Edition 2007

1 3 5 7 9 10 8 6 4 2

Typeset by Julia Lloyd
Printed in the United States of America by Quebecor World Fairfield

To the French, with my sincerest apologies

Photo Acknowledgements

Chapter 1: © Jean Gaumy/Magnum Photos; chapter 2: © Eric Taschaen/epa/Corbis; chapter 3: © Hulton-Deutsch Collection/Corbis; chapter 4: © Rykoff Collection/Corbis; chapter 5: © allactiondigital.com; chapter 6: Annebicque Bernard/Corbis Sygma; chapter 7: © Mike Blenkinsop/ Alamy; chapter 8: Elliott Erwitt/Magnum Photos; chapter 9: © Yves Forestier/Corbis Sygma; chapter 10: © Richard Kalvar/Magnum Photos; chapter 11: Mary Evans Picture Library.

DON'T GET ME WRONG – FRANCE IS A GREAT PLACE to live. It's a country devoted to pleasure. And pleasure is one of my hobbies. No, it's *all* of my hobbies.

But gaining access to that pleasure can sometimes be as fiddly, painful and ultimately frustrating as eating a lobster. You use a hammer, nutcrackers, surgical probes and a laser-powered meat detector, and you can still end up with lacerated fingers and a mouthful of lobster claw.

Many people visiting France, or coming to live here, get stranded in the pre-pleasure and partial-pleasure zones. They get little further than the moody waiter or the rip-off estate agent. They need advice on how to break into the total-pleasure zone. Because living in France is not a gift that you're born with. Lots of French people never learn to do it properly. That's why they're known as a nation of complainers.

Living in France is a skill that you have to work at. I've spent half my adult life here, and I'm still learning.

This book sums up what I've learnt so far.

STEPHEN CLARKE, *Paris*, 2006

CONTENTS

Attentive readers may note that there are eleven, not ten, commandments here. But surely you didn't think you could fit a nation as fascinating and complex as the French into just ten commandments, did you? Merde alors!

Nude pétanque, a French game that gives a whole
new meaning to the phrase 'playing with your boules'.

THE
1ST

COMMANDMENT

Tu Auras Tort

THOU SHALT BE WRONG
(if you're not French)

THOU SHALT BE WRONG
(*if you're not French*)

WHEN DEALING WITH A FRENCHMAN, YOU NEED TO BE aware that there is a voice in his head. It is constantly telling him, 'I'm French, I'm right.'

Even when he's doing something that is quite obviously illegal, antisocial or just plain stupid, he is sure that right is on his side.

Of course, the French aren't unique in this. We Brits think we invented Western civilization. The Americans are convinced that they live in the only place on earth where people are truly free. The Belgians are certain that they invented French fries. We're all sure that we're right about *something*. The difference with the French is that they not only think they're right, they're also convinced that everyone in the world is ganging up to prove them wrong. Why, they wonder, does everyone on the planet want to speak English instead of *le français*?[1] Why does no one else play *pétanque*? Why does the world

. . . .

[1] Just look at the little accent under the c in français and you'll see why. Even the French have trouble spelling French words.

prefer Hollywood blockbusters to French movies about Parisians getting divorced? *Ce n'est pas normal.*

Their reputation for arrogance comes from this. They're not sure of themselves. They've got something to prove to the rest of the universe.

Observe a Parisian driver when he or she comes up against a red light. 'How dare this coloured bulb assume it knows best whether it is safe to cross this junction?' the driver thinks. 'It's obviously safe to go through, there's nothing blocking my way except a few annoying pedestrians.'[2] He ploughs through, certain that the universe is on his side.

It's the same with much of the French service sector. How can the customers possibly be right? What do they know about the service industries?

The list goes on and on.

Pushing L'Enveloppe

One of the best ways of seeing the French person's innate sense of rightness in action is to visit a crowded post office. The people who work here have even more reasons to be right than the rest of their compatriots. They have two layers of rightness that they wear like armour.

First, of course, they are French.

. . . .

[2] The Parisian driver has other reasons to ignore red lights. See the Eighth Commandment.

Second, they are state employees and therefore impossible to fire. Even if they were to snooze all day or feed all the letters through a shredder, the worst sanction they could expect would be a transfer to some distant outpost of the French empire like Tahiti or Calais.

In a relaxed rural post office, this can be to the public's advantage, because the people working there will be able to take the time to help their customers (and thereby show how right they are about things).

But if you walk into a busy urban post office at nine a.m., things might not go so smoothly.

There will probably be a long queue of people wanting to withdraw money from their post-office bank accounts, pay their electricity bills in cash, or simply post a letter because they don't have change for the automatic franking machine.

A post-office cashier who's just coming on duty will enter the room, sum up the size of the queue, see the urgency of opening another window, and smile inwardly. Or sometimes outwardly. He or she will then proceed to interrupt their co-workers' transactions in order to exchange good-morning kisses or handshakes.

Any grumblings from the queue will be answered with a look, or an overt comment, to the effect that, yes, we state workers are human beings and we have the right to greet our colleagues just like anyone else, *non*?

They are in the right and are therefore totally shameless.

Next, the new arrival will sit down at his or her counter and settle in, starting up the computer, slotting in the cash drawer, checking that the books of stamps are all in place.

Any customer who dares to venture from the 'wait behind this line' barrier up to the counter at this point will be politely told that the worker has to get properly prepared before receiving customers. That is normal, *non*? In what other job does a worker have to start work before things are properly prepared?

They are in the right and therefore completely unhurried. The only thing to do is stay patient. It can be tough.

Once, in my local post office, I was praying that fate would not send me to the counter nearest the door, because it was about to be manned by one of the worst cases of 'I'm Right, You're Wrong' I've ever met, even in France.

Monsieur Right was just coming on duty, and was apparently testing his seat for signs of bounciness deficiency that might oblige him to put in for a month's sick leave if he sat on it for a whole morning. He could see all the people waiting, and seemed to be relishing the groans of frustration emanating from his audience. I was next in line, hoping desperately that he'd keep bouncing until one of the other counters was free.

But no, fate decided to be cruel to me that day.

'*Bonjour*,' I said loudly, as you must.

'*Bonjour*,' he replied, slightly put out by my merriness. Outside of the post-office combat zone, I'm sure I would have got on fine with the guy, who was a fairly laid-back, jeans-and-earring type and probably listened to the same kind of music as I do. But on his throne, he was obviously a complete tyrant, the Sun King hoping to burn my fingers.

I told him that my postwoman had left a slip telling me to come to the nearest post office to fetch a parcel, which is the usual practice when a delivery is too big to go in the letter box.

'Do you have ID?' he asked me, which is also the usual practice.

'Yes, I do, but there's a problem. You see, the slip says that the parcel was addressed to Red Garage Books, which is the name of my company. But I don't have an ID card in that name because there is no person called Red Garage Books.' I attempted a little philosophical laugh, which is necessary in France when you want to show people that you are joking.

'Ah,' he said, grimacing as if I'd just pierced his other ear. 'If you have no ID then I can't give you the parcel.'

'But I know it's for me. I'm the only employee. Look, I've brought along a piece of stationery with the logo on it.'

'That is not official ID. I can't accept it.'

'I understand that,' I said, diplomatically acknowledging his rightness. 'But I don't know what else to do. I know what's in the parcel, though. It's books. Can't you just check, please?'

The guy agreed to go and look. These counter assistants are human, after all. And, like all French counter assistants, if you show them – politely – that you aren't going to go away and leave them in peace (yes, two can play at being in the right), they will back down.

He went off backstage with my paper slip. While he

was away, I turned to the people waiting and gave them an apologetic wince. Not too apologetic, though. After all, he was the one who'd gone off. I was in the right.

Eventually, he returned with the package. It was obviously, as I'd told him, a parcel of books. The word '*livres*' was clearly marked on the green customs form stuck on top of the parcel. He looked at the package, at the paper slip, at me, and came to a decision.

'I shouldn't really give this to you, but I'm going to,' he said, putting the parcel on the counter.

'Thank you very much,' I said.

'Sign here.' He gave me the parcel register.

I signed, and as I did so, I saw that the address on the package was in fact 'Stephen Clarke, c/o Red Garage Books, etc'. So it was in my name, after all. The postwoman had got it wrong on her paper slip. I looked up at the counter guy, who had obviously seen this, too, and seemed to be daring me to make an issue of it.

I didn't bother. That postwoman possessed the same two levels of rightness as her colleague behind the counter, so it would have been totally counterproductive to suggest that she'd been in the wrong.

'You must get some ID in your company name to avoid this problem in the future,' he said.

'You are right,' I told him. I gratefully took possession of my parcel, wished him '*bonne journée*' and left.

In France, a tactical retreat is often as close as you get to total victory.

The Right Stuff

Sometimes, the whole world gets things spectacularly wrong.

One of the most traumatic recent examples of this was the day the Olympic Committee announced the host city for the 2012 Games. London? Non! How could the Committee get it so completely wrong? The 2012 Games were destined for Paris, everyone knew that.

Yes, everyone in France. Which, unfortunately for the French, did not include the Olympic Committee.

And what made things even more unbearable in French eyes was that they had lost out to their dreaded rivals, the 'Anglo-Saxons', as they mistakenly call English-speakers. Because, as every French person knows, those evil, globalizing Anglo-Saxons have been leading the conspiracy to prove the French wrong for centuries now ...

In a Breton village called La Masse, on a hilltop near the Mont Saint-Michel, there is what looks like a miniature windmill with its sail jammed in the vertical.[3] This miniature windmill was part of a French communications system that was supposed to revolutionize the world back in the 1790s. It was one of a chain of similar structures on hilltops at fifteen to twenty kilometre intervals

. . . .

[3] On the subject of getting things right, I deliberately phrased that sentence to avoid choosing whether the Mont Saint-Michel is in Brittany or Normandy. Whichever you choose, someone in France will write and tell you you're wrong. So I'm just saying that the village of La Masse is in Brittany, which it undoubtedly is – see the Michelin map number 309 for confirmation. It's a French map, so it must be right.

between Paris and Brest, on the west coast. The sails on top of the buildings were in fact arms that could be moved, semaphore-style, to send a message from Brest to Paris in only twenty minutes. The most frequent message was probably, 'It's really cloudy here in Brittany. If you sent us any messages recently, we didn't get them.'

The system was invented by a French engineer called Claude Chappe, who thoughtfully designed relay stations consisting of two buildings – one for the sending of messages, the other as a dining room for the messengers. Beautifully French.

The idea was simple and yet doomed to obsolescence in a combination that only the French seem to manage. At first, the Chappe telegraph spread outwards from France, with lines even extending as far as Amsterdam and Milan. Then in 1836 a Brit called Charles Wheatstone invented the gloriously simple wire telegraph that was adapted and adopted all over the world, and the French Chappe telegraph was dead. As was poor old Chappe – he killed himself in 1805.

Yes, the French have a perverse gift for inventing things that no other country wants to use, and then brooding about it.

The prime example is the Minitel.

Launched in 1983, it was a forerunner of the Internet. It was a lot like Teletext or Ceefax, except that it was more interactive, and instead of being accessed via a television screen that most households already had, the French complicated things by forcing Minitel users to rent a small dedicated screen.

The Minitel was as slow as all computers were in the eighties, but earned a fortune for France Telecom and the French advertising industry when its sex chat sites caught on. Every billboard, TV channel and magazine in France was suddenly decorated with pouting topless models and Minitel server addresses like 3615 SEXY. Millions of French people spent their nights typing capital-lettered messages on to little fold-down keyboards attached to their cranky beige boxes, and then waiting minutes for the black-and-white screens to refresh themselves and the answers to come back. France, the country that loves conversation more than anything, conceived the online chat room fifteen years before its time.

But then an Englishman called Timothy Berners-Lee invented the World Wide Web to make the American Internet work anywhere, and killed the Minitel. The streets of France were littered with miniature beige screens, and once again those scheming Anglo-Saxons had inflicted a non-French idea upon the world.

Some other examples of this universally unwanted French inventiveness are:

- *Pétanque*, the only sport designed to be played in a dogs' toilet.

- The Citroën DS – shaped like a flattened frog, it is the only road vehicle in the world guaranteed to give all passengers instant carsickness.

- The gear lever on a Renault 4L – perfectly capable of changing gear, but only when it felt like it.

- The primitive soap dispensers that used to be fitted in French café toilets. An oval cake of soap was loaded on to a curved metal bar screwed to the wall above the sink. In theory this was a good idea, as it saved the soap from falling on the floor or melting away in the sink. In practice it was disgusting, because the (usually bright-yellow) cake of soap mostly served as an exhibition space for the yuk that the previous occupant of the toilet had smeared on it. The world was very lucky that the liquid-soap dispenser was invented and killed off the French prototype.[4]

Of course, the French have many reasons to be proud of their creativity, because they have contributed some great inventions to the world – the bikini, scuba diving, Braille, pasteurization, the hot-air balloon (pretty apt, you could say), batteries, the parachute and photography, to name just a few.

And some of their versions of existing technology have become global success stories. Few Americans realize, for instance, that when they take the high-speed train from New York to Boston, they are getting on what is basically a cleverly camouflaged French TGV.[5]

France also conceived some typically French, and very successful, variations on an existing theme:

- The *château*, a building that pretends to have a military function but is in fact merely decorative. A lot like the French army in 1940.

. . . .

[4] For the upside of this bacteria-sharing method, see the Third Commandment on food.

[5] Some American readers might prefer to call this a Freedom train.

- The Foreign Legion, a group of expendable ex-cons and unemployables who can be safely sent into danger zones to do the dirty work. If they don't come back, no influential person is going to kick up a fuss about a lost son.

- Not forgetting the *camping municipal*, that ridiculously cheap (or occasionally free) campsite in countless villages all over France that encourages the passing traveller to stay the night and spend some money in the local café. French hospitality at its best.

But top of this list of inventions that France is right to be proud of has to be a certain edible delicacy.

The farmer who conceived *foie gras* must have been a very inventive Monsieur indeed. You can imagine him explaining his new *pâté* to his friends:

'Oh, you don't just mince up offcuts of meat like you do with other *pâtés*. You take a goose or a duck, stick a funnel down its throat, and pour as much dried maize as you can into its gullet every day until it is so obese it can hardly walk. Then you rip out its grossly deformed liver and spread it on toast.'

'You've been at the absinthe again, Jean-Pierre,' his friends must have said. 'Come and get some fresh air over at the dogs' toilet.'

But old Jean-Pierre was right, and *foie gras* could only have been a French invention. If it had been an Anglo-Saxon idea and called 'fat liver', no one would have bought it.

Am I Right or Am I Right?

The Frenchman's favourite tool when showing how right he is is the rhetorical question. Why is it his favourite tool? Because it emphasizes just how right he is. Why does he use it so often? Because it makes his opinions sound so important that even he has to beg himself to reveal them. Isn't the rhetorical question annoying when it's overused? Yes, it bloody is.

When you arrive in France, if you're not used to the rhetorical question, it can make any kind of serious conversation a farce. You'll be trying to talk about, say, why some new French film is the usual navel-gazing dross about a poor, misunderstood *artiste* who has to smoke a lot and sleep with chic women in fabulous apartments. And at first you will get the impression that your French conversation partner is genuinely interested in what you think of the movie.

'Why is this film almost exactly like his last film?' the French person will ask.

'Perhaps because—' you'll start to answer, but suddenly the French person is drowning you out with their own opinion. And just when you've recovered from your confusion, you hear another question apparently aimed at you.

'And why do young French actresses seem to be contractually obliged to show their boobs?'

'Because—' you begin, but the same thing happens again. And you finally realize that the French person is not asking you a question at all. They're having a conversation with themselves. During which, of course, no one will be able to interrupt them and tell them they're wrong.

The funniest example of this is, apparently, the first day of lectures at Paris's elite school, *Sciences-Po*.[6] It accepts lots of non-French students, who go nervously along to their first lecture, eager to participate in a debate with one of France's most respected intellectuals. Inevitably, when the esteemed professor gets up to speak, he begins to pontificate in a typically French manner.

'And when did France realize that a colonial war in Vietnam was unwinnable?' he will ask the assembled young minds.

Non-French hands will shoot up, their owners keen to play their part in the exchange of ideas that is the very engine-room of French culture.

And they will be ignored, as the professor replies to his own question and moves on to the next one, that again only he has the right to answer.

The foreign students cringe in embarrassment at their intellectual faux pas. Meanwhile, the French students – who know what is (or isn't) expected of them in these lectures – all lounge at the back of the auditorium, taking notes, rolling cigarettes and sending each other text messages along the lines of 'Do you think I'm sexy? Yes you do.'

. . . .

[6] *Po* is short for *politiques*. Yes, a French political-science school, a scary idea.

A Slice of Truth

The big question is, of course, where does this French sense of paranoid rightness come from?[7] Well, I'm no anthropologist or historian, but I think it goes back to 1789 and the Revolution. There is a French verb that means to decide who is wrong and who is right, to make the final decision. It is *trancher*. Not at all coincidentally, this also means to slice or cut off, as in *trancher la tête de quelqu'un* – to cut off someone's head.

Back in 1789, the French started letting the guillotine decide who was right and who was wrong. The king at the time, Louis XVI, was the great-grandson of Louis XIV, the man who had modestly declared himself the Sun King and espoused the theory of the divine right of monarchs to rule over a nation. By Louis XVI's time, this had become the divine right to waste all the country's money on wigs and garden parties.

Some Parisian intellectuals decided enough was enough, so they whipped the people into a frenzy and the guillotine started to make its decisions, first getting rid of the *aristos*, then anyone who dared to challenge the ideas of the clique of intellectuals that happened to be in power on any particular day.

The French Revolution was not just about replacing a monarch with a parliament. It imposed some extreme – not to say traumatic – ideas on the people.

. . . .

[7] I know I just poured scorn on the French habit of asking rhetorical questions, but sometimes they are quite effective. Don't you agree?

For a start, the official language suddenly became French, whereas up until 1789 the vast majority of the nation had been happily speaking its various *patois* and was totally incapable of understanding the language used by the Parisians. When Molière, France's comic Shakespeare, toured the country in the seventeenth century, his troupe of actors often had to resort to putting on slapstick shows because no one could understand their spoken plays.[8] Then suddenly, by decree, the *patois* was banned and everyone had to learn the new 'right' language. Anyone who disagreed had their quarrelsome brain detached from their body.

At the same time, in order to reduce the risk of local dissent, the central government started to displace people around the country. Instead of consisting of regional regiments, the army became a national force, mixing up people from different parts of the country, who were forced, of course, to communicate in French. This kind of thing still happens today, so that someone from Provence who qualifies as a teacher at the university of Nice, and who would love to stay on in their region, stands a very good chance of getting posted to Brittany.

The Republic also imposed a new calendar, with the year starting in September and the months getting descriptive names like *brumaire* ('misty month'), *pluviôse* ('rainy month') and *thermidor* (presumably 'the month in

---

[8] This seems to account for the baffling popularity of *The Benny Hill Show* in France, even today. Three centuries ago, most French people's idea of culture was a bunch of actors and actresses chasing each other around the stage making lewd gestures.

which lobsters are cooked'). Instead of weeks, the months were divided into three ten-day periods, and the ten days were renamed *primidi, duodi, tridi*, and so on, till *decadi*. Yes, the revolutionaries invented the *metric week*.[9]

In any case, what happened in the few years after 1789 was that everyone in the country had their value system cut off like a guillotine victim's head. Everything they'd always assumed to be right was suddenly wrong. If they stayed in their own region, they were told they'd been speaking the wrong language. If they were shunted off to a different region, they were suddenly living like foreigners in their own country, eating the wrong foods, and talking with the wrong accent. In many ways, it's the same experience as being an English expat in France today, and I for one know how disturbing that can be. The sense of alienation tends to push people towards two basic extremes. We expats can end up adopting French culture wholeheartedly, pretending that cricket and Marmite never existed and going to see Johnny Hallyday live at the Stade de France. Or we can cling on desperately to our old truths, and may feel the sudden urge to write to English newspapers about the demise of the unsplit infinitive and the cucumber sandwich. Most expats try out both extremes for a while and then settle about halfway between the two.

As I said, I'm no historian, but it seems to me that

. . . .

[9] And in doing so, seem to have reduced the number of French weekends to three a month. Which may go some way to explaining why Robespierre, the man behind the most radical changes, had his own head removed in 1794. You don't mess with a Frenchman's weekends.

over the two-hundred-odd years since the Revolution, the French seem somehow to have combined these two extreme reactions to being disconnected from their old values. They seem to have embraced the new values (or had them pounded into their brains by the French education system), and then decided that their perfect new way of doing things was under threat, adding the touch of paranoia that they are famous for.

And most of it is the fault of us Anglos. As soon as the French started cutting royalists' heads off, they added a new level of antagonism to their relations with the traditional enemy across the Channel. At first, it was easy for the revolutionaries to sneer at the Brits. Those ridiculous royalist English fops with their mad German monarchs – how could they possibly be right about anything? After all, they had just lost their biggest colony, America, to rebels aided by the French. *Huh*! But things soon started going wrong. Napoleon was beaten at Waterloo and sent to die on a colony that Britain hadn't lost, Saint Helena. And then, just a couple of decades after the French Revolution, how dare these *Anglais* have their own revolution – the industrial one – and start inventing machines that made French technology look outdated? And they even had the effrontery to call one of their first new railway stations *Waterloo*! It was more than enough to make a nation paranoid, *non*?

Things that the French are right about

- An adulterous politician is probably no more corrupt than a monogamous one.

- Just because a man compliments a woman, it doesn't mean that he is planning to rape her.

- Getting out of Vietnam in 1954 was a pretty good idea.

- Invading Iraq was not such a good idea.

- If a country's schoolkids are taught mathematics to a good level, its technology industries will never lack qualified engineers.

- Children do not die if they stop eating French fries for a week.

- Spa holidays should be available as state-subsidized medical treatment.

- If you have a regular office job, there is no point working on Friday afternoons.

- Putting foreign words on menus does not make the food taste better.

- If you invest money in railways, they are more efficient.

- All you need in salad dressing is olive oil, vinegar, mustard and salt. Anything else is window dressing, not salad dressing.

- If the French ignore a European law, no one will be able to force them to obey it.

Things that the French are wrong about

(though it is not wise to tell them so)

- The more you boast about sex, the better you are at it.

- Everyone just adores passive smoking.

- *Pétanque* is a sport.

- Motorway bridges are so beautiful that they must be celebrated on picture postcards.

- The Earth does not revolve around the Sun – it revolves around Paris.

- Benny Hill represents the cutting edge of British comedy.

- The words to a song are so important that you don't need a tune.

- Supertramp are (or were ever) hip.

- If you push in front of someone in a queue, they will respect you more.

- All films should be about the director's love life. (This is why they love Woody Allen so much.)

- It is fun to eat calf's brain and pig's anus.

- Vegetarians cannot have sex.

- Many customers do not actually want to be served.

- Nuclear power is totally unpolluting.

- Johnny Hallyday is world-famous (he's an aging rocker, by the way).

- Serge Gainsbourg was sexy. (He was a chain-smoking, drunk, toad-faced physical wreck. Their best-ever songwriter, though.)

- The louder you laugh at your own joke, the funnier it is.

- France invented French fries. (The whole of the rest of the world accepts that it was either the Belgians or the British.)

- A word does not exist unless it's in the dictionary.

- When there is fog on the motorway, it is safest to drive as fast as you can and get out of the low-visibility zone as quickly as possible.

- Red traffic lights do not always know best about the need to stop.

- Designated flood zones do not flood and are therefore safe to build on.

- You can cure anything by inserting the relevant medicine up your back passage.

- All Americans care enough about France to know where it is on a map of the world.

- All British people are polite.

Phrases that the French use to prove that they are right

(and what the phrases really mean)

Je pense, donc je suis.	*Dje ponce donk dje swee.*	I think therefore I am.

(I think I am right, therefore I am right.)

. . . .

C'est la vie *or* C'est comme ça.	*Say-la vee* or *Say kom sa.*	That's life *or* That's how it is.

(I knew it, and you didn't, so I'm in the right.)

. . . .

C'est cela, oui.	*Say sala wee.*	Yes, that's right.

(No it's not, it is wrong.)

. . . .

Mon oeil.	*Moneu-y.*	My eye.

(An expression of disbelief, a lot like the English phrase.)

. . . .

Mon cul, oui.	*Monkoo wee.*	My arse.

(An extremely rude expression of disbelief, like the English equivalent.)

. . . .

Et mon cul, c'est du poulet?	*Ay monkoo say doo poolay?*	And my arse is chicken, is it?

(An even ruder expression of disbelief.)

CONTINUED...

Ah bon?	Ahbo?	Really?

(Not really at all. You are talking bullshit. Or: Really? That's totally ridiculous.)

. . . .

J'ai raison.	Djay rayzo.	I am right.

(Literally 'I have reason', implying that someone who is wrong is
not only wrong but also crazy.)

. . . .

Vous avez tort.	Voozavay tor.	You are wrong.

(An expression closely related to the word tordu, meaning twisted, so that to
a Frenchman being wrong is basically equivalent to being a pervert.)

. . . .

Je suis moyennement d'accord.	Dje swee moi-yennmo dakor.	I am averagely in agreement.

(I disagree totally.)

. . . .

Mais j'ai le droit de . . .	May djay l'drwa da.	But I have the right to . . .

(. . . and insert whatever unreasonable thing you have just done
and are desperately trying to justify.)

. . . .

Vous vous prenez pour qui?	Voovoo pr'nay porky.	Who do you think you are?

(Someone who is more right than me? Huh!)

. . . .

Je vous l'avais dit.	Dje voo lavay dee.	I told you so.

(So I'm doubly right. Not only am I right, I'm right about being right.)

A useful phrase when dealing with a French person who knows they're right but may just be wrong

(and what it really means)

| Ah oui, vous avez raison. | *Ah wee voozavay rayzo.* | Ah yes, you are right. |

(OK, *you win, but that doesn't mean to say I'm going to disappear out of your life and let you get away without helping me out here,* mon ami.)

The French protesting after being told that they
will have to work on Friday afternoons.

THE
2ND
COMMANDMENT

Tu Ne Travailleras Pas
THOU SHALT NOT WORK

THOU SHALT NOT WORK

'LIFE IS NOT WORK. WORKING TOO MUCH SENDS YOU INSANE.' That was said not by a French anarchist, artist or aristocrat, but by a president, Charles de Gaulle, to André Malraux, a former minister of culture. Quite a political statement.

The French say that they work to live, whereas Anglo-Saxons live to work. What they mean is, while we think that getting into the office at five a.m., skipping lunch and staying on till midnight to close that deal with New York is a virtue, the French have better things to do.

And they're right. Given the choice, who wouldn't agree to earn less money if it meant that they got the chance to lie in for two extra hours in the morning, enjoy a long gourmet lunch, and then spend the evening nibbling at the earlobe (and other nibblable bits) of their loved one?

This is exactly why I came to live in France. I was working for a British company that regularly offered me promotions and rises, and I felt very proud of myself until I noticed that I didn't have weekends or evenings any more and couldn't remember what my girlfriend looked like. Mainly because I was drinking so much as soon as I left the office that most evenings were a blur.

I took a job in France with less stress, less responsibility and less money, and immediately clicked into the French philosophy: hard work is just too much hard work.

Très Long Weekend

Looking in a French diary, you might get the impression that no one in the country is ever at work. Trying to phone an office on a Friday afternoon will usually confirm this.

French workers get the following bank holidays: New Year's Day, Easter Monday, 1 May, VE Day (8 May), Ascension Day, Pentecost Monday (the first Monday in June), Bastille Day (14 July), Assumption Day (15 August), All Saints' Day (1 November), 1918 Armistice Day (11 November) and Christmas Day. In a bad year, 1 and 8 May can fall on a weekend and aren't replaced by a weekday off. But in a good year, they might fall on a Tuesday, so that workers will take a *pont* (a 'bridge', an extra day off to make it a long weekend). That way, the first and second weekends in May and the Ascension Day weekend (between mid-May and mid-June) will be four days long, and then Pentecost Monday could make it four long weekends out of six. In a good year, the French take almost as many days off in May and June as some Americans get in a year – and still have almost all their holiday to take.

Most French people in full-time work get five weeks' paid holiday a year. Some get even more – in my last journalism job, the company gave us thirty-seven days a year – seven and a half weeks. (All this on top of the bank holidays, remember.)

This calendar, combined with the 'work to live, don't live to work' attitude, can lead the French to take what you might call a relaxed attitude to work. By Friday lunchtime, they'll be mentally engrossed in their weekend. Come May, it's almost summer so there's no point over-exerting themselves.

But if you work with the French, this isn't necessarily a problem. When they are actually working, they're very productive. You just have to choose the right time to ask them to do something. Don't bother trying to get anything done between twelve and two p.m. on any day, at any time after eleven a.m. on a Friday, or between 1 May and 31 August. Simple, really.

God Save the Thirty-Five-Hour Week

The working week was reduced from thirty-nine to thirty-five hours in France in 2000, but this didn't mean that all full-time workers suddenly stopped an hour early every day. Companies introduced the policy after negotiation with their workers. Some firms settled on five seven-hour days, others gave a half-day off per week or a day off every fortnight.

My employer gave us the time as holiday – an extra

twenty-two days a year. This meant that I now had fifty-nine days' leave a year, plus eleven bank holidays – a total of fourteen weeks per year.

All this, I should add, with no reduction in salary.

When I boasted to friends and family, I could feel the waves of jealousy flooding across the Channel and the Atlantic.[10]

Contrary to popular opinion amongst employers, the idea of the thirty-five-hour week was not to bankrupt all of France's businesses. It was to create jobs – since the working week had been reduced by about 10 per cent, logically, a team of ten people would now need one new colleague to make up the hours. Companies were promised large subsidies to take on 10 per cent more staff, and the government hoped to create seven hundred thousand jobs this way.

This worked fine for companies with lots of people doing the same job, but I was working for a magazine with a staff of ten. To make up our lost hours, our new recruit would have had to be 10 per cent editor, 20 per cent writer, 20 per cent designer, etc, etc.

In practice, we didn't get any new recruits. We were told that we would all have to become 10 per cent more efficient during our reduced work time. Which we did. It's not hard to become more productive if the incentive is twenty-two days' extra holiday a year.

An OECD report said that productivity in France went

....

[10] With typical Anglo-Saxon ingratitude, this was when I decided to start writing books poking fun at the French.

up 2.32 per cent between 1996 and 2002, compared with only 1.44 per cent in the rest of the EU. And four of those years were before the thirty-five-hour week was introduced. If you took just 2000–2002, once the thirty-five-hour week had begun, I'm sure the results would be even more startling.

As I said, the French work to live. Or, more precisely, they work to go on holiday. A French worker won't bust their gut to be voted employee of the month and get their mugshot on the wall. But promise them enhanced lifestyle time, and they can work wonders.

'Anglo-Saxon' economists predict meltdown if a similar scheme were to be introduced in their countries. And they might be right. Because there is one major difference between the French and Anglo-Saxons.

Give a Frenchman a long weekend and he'll get in his French car, fill it with French petrol, drive to the French seaside, countryside or mountains, and spend three or four days eating and drinking French food and wine. Give a Brit the same opportunity and he'll get in an Irish jet and fly to Bulgaria.

The French travel abroad a lot, but a massive amount of their money stays at home. It seems too good to be true, but it is true – working less is good for the French economy.

The End of the Thirty-Five-Hour Week?

Under pressure from employers who say they're paying a full-time salary for part-time work, and from right-wing politicians who say that the Anglo-Saxon model of over-work is good for the soul, the French government recently authorized companies to abolish the thirty-five-hour week. But everyone knows that any attempt to take rights away from French workers results in a national strike, so the increase in worktime is being dealt with in a typically French way. Employers will have to negotiate the increase with their employees, who can refuse and remain on thirty-five hours. And if the full-time working week is increased to thirty-nine hours again, employers will have to *buy back* the hours at the employees' rate of salary. In other words, the employer will have to offer four hours' pay, or a 10 per cent rise.

And that's supposed to be good for the employers?

A State of Mind

The people with the worst reputation for being relaxed during office hours are the *fonctionnaires*, the state workers. French comedian Coluche used to tell a joke: 'My mum was a *fonctionnaire*, and my dad didn't work either.'

The *fonctionnaires* include teachers, the police, hospital workers, firefighters, all civil servants in government offices and researchers in state institutes. Post-office and transport workers are not exactly *fonctionnaires*, but have similar rights and are so numerous that they have as much power over the government as *fonctionnaires* do.

Official statistics put the number of *fonctionnaires* at around 3.3 million. But one French magazine recently estimated that *fonctionnaires* or semi-*fonctionnaires* make up just over a quarter of the French workforce – six million workers. Whatever the figure, any government tries to reform the *fonction publique* at its peril. If it announces a plan to meddle with the *éducation nationale*, for example, there are not only a couple of million workers to go on strike, there are also all the students, who enjoy nothing better than a bit of educational rioting to prepare them for adult life.

And the worst *fonctionnaires* often have the best careers. It is well known that the only way to get rid of a totally inefficient *fonction publique* manager is to promote them so that they go and annoy a bigger department.

Fonctionnaire secretaries are the same. A friend of mine, a researcher, had a secretary who brought a TV into her office so that she could watch dubbed American soap operas in the afternoon. He complained to the head of department, who said there was nothing that could be done – if they annoyed her, all the secretaries in the institute would go on strike. My friend suffered for two years until he finally found another researcher who did so little work that he didn't notice for six months that his previous secretary had retired. The TV-watcher filled that vacancy and my friend was saved.

Similarly, if the director of a school wants to get rid of

a teacher who shows DVDs every lesson, gets drunk every lunchtime and regularly comes back two weeks late after the summer break, they will have to offer the offender a transfer to a school in a more prestigious part of France. I spent a year working as an English assistant in a *lycée* in Perpignan, and although some of the English teachers did give a damn about the kids, several others were only there for the Pyrenees skiing and the Mediterranean watersports. One typical lesson I attended involved the teacher putting on a Charlie Chaplin video (great for improving their English conversation skills), yelling at his pupils to shut up, and going to the staffroom for a smoke. *Très éducatif*. And the only thing that the school director could have done was try to persuade him to transfer to Saint-Tropez.

The *fonctionnaires* defend themselves by saying that in exchange for their jobs for life they get low pay and little chance of promotion. But the *fonction publique* can't be that bad – a recent opening for an administrative assistant at the state's institute for population studies, a job that did not even require the *baccalauréat* (equivalent to A levels), attracted more than eighty applicants, including several with doctorates.

A stress-free job is a temptation that no French person can resist.

Jobs for the Garçons

Given all these incentives to laze about at work, it's a wonder that the French get anything done. But they do. Without making a fuss, they build bridges, motorways, railways, whole new towns, with incredible speed.

Part of the reason for this is that they don't really listen to environmental opposition. So what if a few sandal-wearing tree-lovers don't want the new TGV line to slice through their valley? People need to get to the beach or the ski resorts quickly. So the new line gets built in less time than it takes to fix a date for an initial public inquiry in Britain.

Another reason is that major building projects are kept in the French family.

Compare, for example, France's and England's national stadiums. The French decided to build a new stadium for the 1998 World Cup, so they gave the job to French firms and it was finished in January, six months before the tournament began. England decided it needed a new stadium, knocked down the old one, outsourced the building work to a foreign firm[11] and immediately lost all control of the budget and deadline. The result – it was late and turned out to be the most expensive stadium in world history.

Vive la méthode française.

....

[11] When I explain this to French people, they think it is very funny that we English outsourced our national stadium to our arch sporting rivals, the Australians. I have trouble convincing them that it is not an English joke.

Inefficient Efficiency

We Anglo-Saxons are forever giving ourselves targets. This makes us feel very efficient, even if we fail to meet them. Yes, we boast, we have increased the number of daily targets by 10 per cent. OK, we missed 90 per cent of those targets, but by setting ourselves more targets tomorrow we will improve our target-setting efficiency, *and* produce lots of lovely Powerpoint graphs.

The French give themselves far fewer targets at work, for two main reasons.

First, they spend their whole time at school haunted by targets. Every single thing they do there is graded out of twenty and recorded on a report card. By the time they get to work they're traumatized by targets.

Second, they daren't give themselves too many targets because they know they will miss them.[12] But perversely, this lack of goals doesn't make them less efficient.

Look at the fuss caused by the British obsession with the first-class post. There are probably more British post-office workers studying how to deliver first-class letters on time than there are delivering letters.

The French have two classes of letter, too, but they don't care about their 'first class' (or *tarif normal*, as they modestly call it) letters arriving within twenty-four hours. French businesses get on with opening the letters they have actually received that morning rather than

....

[12] For the Stade de France, the deadline was imposed by someone else – FIFA. It wasn't self-imposed.

worrying about the ones that might be on their way.

The Brits are so obsessed with performance statistics that performance actually gets worse. I was recently on a train from London to Luton Airport. I wanted to get off at St Albans, midway along the route. But when we got to the first stop outside Central London, it was announced that because the train was running ten minutes late it would be going direct to Luton Airport so as not to miss its performance target. I, and most of the other passengers, had to get off and wait twenty minutes for the next train. The result: the train was on time but the passengers were late. A stroke of British management genius.

A French train, even one of the slightly worse-for-wear ones on the Paris suburban lines, would never do this. It would trundle on to the terminus, running a few minutes late, and the commuters would finish their newpapers, send a few extra text messages, and not care a bit about the ten minutes they had theoretically lost.

French trains do break down and they can be disastrously late, but over all they are much more efficient than British trains, and I'm sure it's because the French railways spend less of their resources on studying lateness and more on trains.

Meeting of Minds (and Tongues)

Until I came to work in France, I was under the naïve impression that meetings were meant to produce decisions.

I quickly learned that the purpose of a French meeting is to listen to oneself (and, if absolutely necessary, others) talk. If you want to reach a decision then you'll have to arrange another meeting.

At the press group where I worked, all meetings were given a start and end time, and woe betide anyone who tried to finish a meeting early. If a meeting to discuss, say, the name of a new magazine was scheduled to last two hours, there was no way that a brilliant name suggested ten minutes into the discussion was ever going to be adopted.

This happened once at a meeting I was actually chairing, and I managed to end the proceedings less than half an hour after they had got under way. When my boss found out about this premature evacuation of the meeting room, she insisted that we hold another meeting to talk about whether we had come to the right decision.

Our meetings rarely had an agenda, and if they did it was almost always ignored. We would get to item two of ten, someone would start philosophizing about an idea they had had while staring at the numbers on the agenda, and suddenly we were so far away from the supposed subject that we would never get back on track. Items three to ten would be forgotten for ever.

Not that this made us less efficient. Sometimes, I

realized, it is best not to make decisions. By the time we finally got round to trying to resolve a problem, it would have either solved itself or become irrelevant. It is better to have no decision at all than a wrong or hasty decision.

Again, French 'inefficiency' is actually more efficient. *Vive l'inaction*.

I Strike, Therefore I Am

In my novel A *Year in the Merde*, there is a running joke that lots of people take seriously. Instead of a *plat du jour*, a dish of the day, there's the *grève du mois*, the strike of the month. Everyone's at it – transport workers, the police, waiters, pharmacists, even porn actors. This was meant to be an exaggeration of what it feels like living in strike-torn France, and attentive readers might have noticed how coincidental it is that in the chapter about Paul West's battle against dog poo, the street cleaners down brushes, condemning Paul's shoes to an even thicker coating of *caca*.

Attempted satire aside, it is true that the French strike a lot. And the reason is obvious – their strikes work spectacularly well.

One of the main reasons is that instead of a stoppage by the Union of Left-handed Carburettor Polishers, a whole industry or the entire country will go on strike at once, so the government and employers almost always back down.

Union members in any industry, in any company, will

probably belong to one of five big unions – the CGT (Confédération Générale du Travail), FO (Force Ouvrière), CFDT (Confédération Française Démocratique du Travail), CFTC (Confédération Française des Travailleurs Chrétiens) and Sud, a new and powerful breakaway from the CFDT. If, for example, the CGT calls all its members out, it can paralyse trains, buses, factories, hospitals, power stations and TV channels (which is sometimes no bad thing).

Often, the only things weakening the strikes are the unions themselves, as they are fierce rivals. So a Paris transport strike can be undermined if all the CFDT drivers stop work but the Sud members turn up out of spite.[13]

The reasons for strikes are sometimes purely symbolic. Train drivers will decide, for example, that the government should do more to improve the lot of the ordinary worker, and will call a one-day strike (thereby depriving the ordinary worker of a day's pay). Some people say that one of the reasons why Paris lost the 2012 Olympics was that, on the day the Olympic Committee was visiting the city, Paris transport workers came out on a twenty-four-hour strike. The city authorities begged the unions to postpone their day of action, but were told that it would be too complicated to re-schedule.

....

[13] In fact, only around 8 per cent of the French workforce belong to a union, but the unions are very good at latching on to any industrial dispute and taking it over. And naturally, when there is a strike, the media call up the union spokesperson, not the factory workers who have a grievance, so the unions feel a lot more powerful than they really are.

The strike went ahead, the Olympic Committee saw a paralysed transport system, and London got the Games.

There is almost always a city in France without public transport because of a strike. Paris is usually hit as soon as the weather starts getting bad in winter. The reasons vary – sometimes it is because drivers are being attacked on suburban lines and want more protection. At other times it is just because the transport workers want to show how powerful they are.

Whatever the reason, though, commuters are remarkably tolerant. For the first couple of days there is total anarchy, with fights breaking out as people getting off buses stomp on the heads of people getting on – but then things settle down and a sort of resigned solidarity kicks in. People without access to a car start to hitchhike to work, get their bikes out of the cellar, or simply walk. And when interviewed by TV reporters, they will often say that they support the strikers. Any strike for workers' rights ultimately protects all the workers.

Plus, of course, if there's a strike by one group of workers, *everyone* has a good excuse for working less.

Striking a Blow

Big national strikes are usually a cause for celebration. The strikers take to the streets and it's carnival time. The unions unfurl their banners and get out the recruitment leaflets. Train- and bus-loads of singing, laughing, face-painted strikers migrate to the big cities[14] and the streets echo to the howl of megaphones and the squeaking of union leaders' scalps as their heads swell along with their new public profile. Cafés along the route of the march make a fortune, and the demonstrators' eyes water at the paraffin smoke billowing out from the *merguez* (North African spicy sausage) stands that line the route.

At the end of the demonstration, as the media are always keen to show, people's eyes can start watering for a different reason. Recently, French protest marches have tended to end in clouds of tear gas and baton charges. This is not because strikers lose their temper – strikes, as I said, are more about carnival than carnage – but because big crowds attract gangs of so-called *casseurs*. These 'breakers', or vandals, are usually kids from the poor outer suburbs of the city, who see the protest march as an opportunity to loot shops, steal mobile phones from posh middle-class protesters and throw things at the police.

At the end of the demonstration (which always finishes at a pre-determined place), the protesters disperse to catch their trains and buses home or go for a self-congratulatory drink, and the *casseurs* take over. The plain-clothes policemen in the crowd wade in, make some media-friendly arrests by dragging young men across the tarmac by their hair, the riot police do their gladiator thing, and the world media have their 'Paris under siege' headline.

....

[14] Coincidentally, the trains and buses bringing strikers to the demonstrations are never held up by strikes.

But, like everything in French society, these riots are stage-managed. Canny protesters get well out of the way before the riot begins. Local residents park their cars a few streets away. Shopkeepers lower their shutters. Many protest groups now hire their own security to identify and take out the *casseurs*. And recent student demonstrations have been patrolled by the young people's parents, babysitting the protest march. Nothing must spoil the carnival.

Wagging the Chien

One of the reasons why the French feel a sense of worker solidarity even during a long transport strike is that they feel such a passionate hatred for their bosses, *les patrons*.

Since the revolutionaries decapitated the aristocracy, France has had plenty of time to create a new elite. And this elite does everything it can to distance itself from the grubby people on the production line. TF1, France's biggest commercial TV station, wanted to make a reality TV series in which a company chairman would spend a day doing the most menial job in his company. But they could not find a single volunteer amongst French *patrons*. In the end, they had to use a Belgian.

A French chairman demean himself by doing hands-on work for a day? *Pas possible!*

Despite French scoffing at the British class system, which school you went to is infinitely more important in France than in the UK. How many of Britain's top business people went to Eton or Oxford? Hardly any. In France, on the other hand, both the private and public sector are basically run by graduates of the ENA (Ecole Nationale d'Administration), the school that turns out the country's top civil servants.

I have heard countless people moaning that their department has just been handed over to a young *Enarque* (ENA graduate) who knows absolutely nothing about the business and who immediately sets about sabotaging perfectly good working practices by applying the outdated theory he has just learned at school. The most important subject in the French curriculum is mathematics, so in general the ability to do complicated calculations and produce pretty graphs is considered much more useful than a true knack for business.

Most recent presidents of France have come from the ENA, which explains why they seem to know nothing about running a country – a lot like monarchs, in fact. The French recognize this. I have heard a joke variously aimed at the ENA, the HEC (Haute Ecole de Commerce), France's most prestigious, incredibly expensive business school, and the Ecole Polytechnique, the top engineering school. For the sake of argument I'll aim it at the ENA. The joke goes something like this:

> There's a rowing race between ENA graduates and a team of ordinary workers, ten rowers to each boat. The first time they race, the workers win by half a length. The ENA does a study, decides that its team lacked leadership and replaces two of the rowers in the boat with a

Rowing Director and a Rowing Coach.

In the second race, the ENA loses by three lengths. The ENA does another study and concludes that the eight rowers were not motivated enough. Three of them are replaced by a Team Leader, a Team Liaison Manager and a Rowing Quality Control Manager. There are now only five rowers left, with five managers.

In the third race, the ENA loses by twenty lengths, and decides that its whole rowing system needs a fundamental review. All the remaining rowers are replaced by auditors.

In the last race, the ENA boat does not even move. The auditors declare that rowing is not a worthwhile activity and should be stopped immediately. The ENA graduates don't care – they are given fat bonuses and sent to improve efficiency somewhere else.

Fortunately, after a few years of trying to reform things, these ENA types seem to settle down to a life of endless meetings and even more endless lunches, and leave the lower ranks to get on with running the business.

Grown-up Schoolboys

It's not only graduates of the elite schools who like to put the 'Education' section at the top of their CV.

The reason so many young people leave France is that they can't get a job unless they have a certificate – *diplôme* – proving they can do it.

At the magazine I worked for in Paris, only one of six English-language journalists had a degree in journalism. This was because we Anglos were outside the French system. It was well known in the company that no French candidates for a magazine job would even get an interview if they didn't have the name of a journalism school on their CV.

New recruits to all departments were announced in a *note bleue* – a memo printed on blue paper. One *note bleue*, announcing the arrival of a thirty-eight-year-old marketing director, began with the words 'Olivier Whatsisnom has a diploma in international marketing from the Ecole de . . .' I could hardly believe it – at thirty-eight, his business-school degree was still more important than the actual business he'd done since.

In the eyes of a French human-resources officer, even if someone has set up their own company, made a small fortune and sold out to a multinational, their experience will not count for as much as a two-year course at a business school.

Phrases you will hear when talking to a relaxed French worker who does not want to deal with your problem

Il/elle ne répond pas. Rappelez lundi/en septembre.	*Eel/ell n'raypo pa. Rapalay lundee/o septombra.*	He/she is not answering. Call back on Monday/ in September.
Je vous repasse le standard.	*Dje voo repass l'stondar.*	I'll put you through to the switchboard again.
Je suis désolé, nous allons fermer.	*Dje swee dayzolay, noo zallo fair may.*	Sorry, we're about to close.
Vous auriez dû vous en occuper plus tôt.	*Voo zoriay doo voozon okupay pluto.*	You should have tried to sort this out earlier.
Ce n'est pas mon problème, Monsieur/Madame.	*Snay pa mo prob-lemm, M'syeu/Mad-am.*	It's not my problem, Sir/Madam.
Ce n'est vraiment pas de ma faute.	*Snay vraymo pa d'ma fot.*	It's really not my fault.
Vous avez fait un mauvais numéro.	*Voozavay fay uh mo-vay noomayro.*	You dialled the wrong number.
Restez poli, quand même. Au revoir.	*Restay polly ko-mem. Aura vwa.*	There's no call to be rude. Goodbye.

Phrases you might need to say when dealing with the relaxed French worker

Non, ne raccrochez pas.	*No, n'rakrochay pas.*	No, don't hang up.
Mais c'est le standard qui m'a mis en communication avec vous.	*May say la stondar ki ma mee-o komunikashon avek voo.*	But it was the switchboard that put me through to *you*.
Ma vie et celle de toute ma famille sont entre vos mains.	*Ma vee ay sell d'toot ma fammee so tontra vo-ma.*	My life and that of my entire family is in your hands.
D'accord, je rappelerai lundi/ en septembre.	*Dakor, dje rapelleray lundee/o septombra.*	OK, I'll call back on Monday/in September.
Vous êtes un vrai connard/une vraie connasse.	*Vooz ett uh vray konar/oon vray konass.*	You are a real bastard/ bitch.

(NB: *this is only to be used if you never intend contacting the person again, and if you're sure they won't be able to trace your call.*)

It is a well-known fact that on the French section of the front line,
the Battle of the Somme was stopped for lunch.

THE
3RD
COMMANDMENT

Tu Mangeras
THOU SHALT EAT

THOU SHALT EAT

I F THE BIBLE HAD BEEN WRITTEN BY A FRENCHMAN, THERE would have been a lot more recipes in it. And this would have been the first commandment.

You can't live in France if you're not interested in food. The French do not respect people who deny themselves any pleasure at all, and, despite what they might try to tell the world, they take food even more seriously than sex. So someone who is not able to groan orgasmically at the mere mention of pigs' entrails is roughly equivalent to an impotent monk. And vegetarians are regarded with extreme suspicion, like a guest at a jacuzzi orgy who stays dry and fully clothed, with his back to all the action and his ears plugged.

The French do, of course, have a lot to get excited about. Ever since the first Neolithic tribes became sedentary in France, people have been spending their time dreaming up ways of preparing, cooking and preserving everything that the land, sea and air had to offer. Those TV documentaries that re-create the lives of Stone-Age peoples probably don't apply to the French at all. Instead of grunting as they chewed through shape-less, blackened hunks of mammoth, the Stone-Age Frenchmen would have spent hours discussing what sauce to use, how long to cook the meat, and on what sized flame.

It's no coincidence that the best Neolithic cave paint-ings in Europe are in central France. All those sketches of woolly mammoths were serving suggestions.

They would probably have got a lot more nourish-ment out of the mammoth, too. Whereas the Stone-Age Brits would have eaten the meatiest bits and fed the rest to their domesticated wolves, the French would have consumed all the organs, including the lungs and the brain, and every bit of the limbs, right down to the jelly inside the hooves (or whatever kind of feet mam-moths have). They would then have made sauces out of any leftovers, to give a bit more flavour to the half-edible bits of the next animal they killed.

Hardly surprising that they didn't have time to build Stonehenge.

Life Is a Finger Buffet

The French have retained some of their Stone-Age culi-nary traditions, and often display what looks like a total lack of hygiene. Food is manhandled, cheeses are sold when their rinds are mouldy, meat and eggs are eaten half-cooked or raw. Early-morning deliveries of food to restaurants are often left outside on the pavement, where, as everyone knows, dogs commonly leave unhygienic deposits.

In short, the French believe that bacteria have the right to live and breed, preferably in people's stomachs.

Bread seems to be the biggest vector of germs. You can watch a *boulangère* squeeze a baguette, enjoying the crunch it makes, accept payment with the same hand, rummage around in her cash drawer, and then transfer all the bacteria in her coin collection to the next baguette – yours.

It is common to see waiters or cooks carrying an armful of unwrapped baguettes through the streets, or pulling an open trolley of bread. When the loaves get to the restaurant, they are often cut into slices by the waiters, who also handle money. The baskets of bread will be served at one table, fondled by the customers there, taken back to the breadboard, and leftover chunks of baguette will be used to fill up other baskets. So the piece of bread with which you soak up the vinaigrette on your plate might well have been squeezed by a *boulangère*, rubbed under a waiter's armpit, fingered by a previous diner, and maybe even dropped on the café floor, before you pop it into your mouth. Yummy.

Even more appetizing – in cafés, you occasionally get a glass that smells of secondhand beer, probably because after it was last used it was just quickly swilled out with the upward-squirting glass rinser behind the bar. You have to hope that the previous drinker didn't have gum disease.

And yet all this doesn't seem to do anyone any harm. There are hardly any outbreaks of salmonella or E. *coli* poisoning in France[15] and food allergies are almost unheard of.

An English expat in France once told me what happened when she'd eaten a snack with traces of peanuts in it. She'd started to swell up and get short of breath, and was afraid she was going to die. When the ambulancemen arrived, she told them '*Je suis allergique aux cacahuètes*' – I am allergic to peanuts – and they burst out laughing. In their defence, the sentence does sound absurd in French. It would be like telling English ambulancemen that 'My ketchup was radioactive.'

In the end, she was only saved because her mother, anticipating trouble, had found a technical name for nut allergy in a medical encyclopedia and written it down.[16] The French can't resist scientific names, which make everything sound more official, and the English girl's password earned her a life-saving injection.

Every year, the country is swept by epidemics of gastroenteritis, but the French seem to regard these as rites of passage. The body gets sick, poops out the virus, and is stronger. A bit of disease is good for the digestion.

This is why on French beaches you see more adults than children with little fishing nets. The grown-ups are

. . . .

[15] Admittedly, this lack of public epidemics may have more to do with France's love of secrecy – see the Seventh Commandment.

[16] *Allergie aux arachides* ('al air-djee o'zarasheed'). Ideally, if they had enough breath left, the patient would say, '*J'ai une allergie aux arachides et je suis en choc anaphylactique*' ('djay oon al air-djee o'zarasheed ay dje swee o'shock anna flak teek'), basically explaining that they have this allergy and can't breathe very well.

collecting shrimps from the rock pools, even on beaches in the centre of large resorts where the seawater might not be exactly clean enough to pickle your olives in. They will also pull mussels off the rocks, and anything that looks like an oyster will be taken back to the kitchen in a bucket and slurped down raw.

A resultant bout of food poisoning, which would scare most people off seafood for life, will be regarded as a bit of bad luck. A French friend of mine who spent a week vomiting after a mussel-gathering trip in Normandy was astonishingly philosophical about her experience: 'The sewage outflow was round the other side of the headland, so we thought they'd be OK,' she said. 'My grandparents have been eating those mussels for years, and they never get sick.' Sewage as vaccine. Not everyone's cup of tea, even in France.

The French Get Fresh

British and American supermarkets have made a lot of progress since grapes used to come individually wrapped in cling film and the only homegrown fruit you saw were a few embarrassed-looking, over-polished apples. These days, farmers' markets are reminding us Anglo-Saxons that food often comes from the ground rather than factories. But French markets don't need to call themselves 'farmers' markets'. Even the most urban Parisian market looks as if it has one foot out in the countryside.

This is because the French still love eating fresh, seasonal produce. Like anywhere else in Europe, you can buy artificially ripened Spanish strawberries in the heart of winter, but come summer, the market stalls explode with Gariguette strawberries – long, pinkish-red, extra-juicy fruit with a flavour you just don't get from the winter version.

A French summer holiday, especially in the southwest, has a bright-orange tinge to it – the colour of the flesh of Charentais melons. At many markets there will be stalls selling nothing else. To test whether they're ripe you don't squeeze them – you sniff their bottoms, doggy-style. Ripe ones smell of sweet melon (logical, really). And if they're fully ripe, their flesh will be deep, dark orange and taste almost as if it were already laced with port.

A few weeks later, the figs start to arrive. The gooey red insides of a green fig, ripe to the point of eruption, are like naturally occurring jam – juicier and sweeter than any fruit you will find in the northern hemisphere at that time of year.

It's the same for the purple Muscat grapes that are dusty-looking and a million times softer than the crisp, shiny, almost transparent torpedoes that are usually sold in English supermarkets. Squeezing them into your mouth is like drinking virgin wine.

The first days of autumn bring a muddy, smoky-smelling invasion of fresh fungus to every vegetable stall in France. Some are from the Chernobyl zone, but plenty of them have been delivered straight from French forests, just begging to be cleaned, fried in butter and enfolded in an omelette, providing one of the most erotic experiences you can have with an egg since a soft-porn film I once saw called something like *Things to Do with a Yolk*. But the mushroom-omelette experience is, if anything, even more pleasurable because it's only possible for the few weeks when the best mushrooms are in town.

Not only is this food all seasonal, but it has often travelled just a short distance, so it's extremely fresh. In many regions of the country, when you go to a restaurant, you can get a meal whose ingredients, apart from the citrus fruits, coffee and sugar, all come from within fifty kilometres of where you're sitting.

The île de Ré, near La Rochelle, is my favourite place for this. The nineteen-mile-long island produces masses of seafood, all kinds of vegetables, its own wine, beer, meat, butter, cheese and more. Half a dozen fresh local oysters and a glass of the island's white wine is one of the best snacks you could ever wish for, and will cost less than the price of a railway sandwich.

To put it simply, we Anglo-Saxons may have lots of celebrity chefs, but the French have celebrity *food*. I know which I prefer.

French Women Do Get Fat

A glance at the bodies on an average French beach will disprove the theory that French women don't get fat. The same goes for men and children. There are plenty of people in France who have fallen victim to the attractions of the junk-food, no-exercise diet.

But over all, the French do get less fat than others. *Mais pourquoi?*

Here is a typical week's worth of midday meals served at a certain Parisian establishment. Read it and try to guess who was eating this food.

MONDAY
Beetroot salad with croutons, lamb couscous with semolina and boiled vegetables, sweetened yoghurt, seasonal fruit.

TUESDAY
Grated carrot salad with lemon-juice dressing, roast pork with mustard sauce, peas, Gruyère cheese, fromage blanc with fruit in syrup.

WEDNESDAY
Lettuce and avocado, fried steak with flageolet beans, Saint-Nectaire cheese, fruit cocktail.

THURSDAY
Potato salad with tarragon, turkey curry with green beans, Pyrenean cheese, seasonal fruit.

FRIDAY
Carrot, cabbage and sweetcorn salad, cod in hollandaise sauce, rice with vegetables, Camembert, chocolate cream.

So who was eating these lunches? The regulars at a *menu fixe* restaurant? The workers in one of Paris's museums? The staff of Air France?

No, it's a typical week's worth of canteen menus in the schools of Paris's 4th *arrondissement*.

On only one day, a Thursday late in the month, were French fries on the menu. On only two days was there no fresh salad as a starter, and that was because it was replaced once by a soup and once by an onion tart. On eleven days, the dessert was a seasonal fruit.[17]

The French don't need a celebrity chef to tell their schools how to feed kids. And they are strong believers in educating the taste buds of the young generation. Not just to ensure future customers for French farmers, but also to try and make sure that the kids don't turn into three-hamburgers-a-day food yobs.

Make no mistake, French kids love to go to fast-food places, and dream of having French fries with every meal. But schools are places where you're supposed to learn *les bonnes manières*, and that includes the 'right' diet. The menus aren't monastic – there are lots of sugary desserts – but they are obligatory (except for religious variants), and educate the palate just as compulsory long division shapes the mind. There are probably more herbs, spices and types of cheese in a month's school menus than some American children eat in a lifetime.

French adults carry on this meal-eating habit gained in youth. Office workers rarely gobble a sandwich at their desk. The majority of office workers I've dealt with

. . . .

[17] The *arrondissement*'s menus are published monthly on its website. Go to http://www.mairie4.paris.fr/mairie4/jsp/Portail.jsp?id_page=86 and click on one of the links under the heading *Menus de la Caisse des Ecoles*.

will go and have a sit-down meal at lunchtime, either at their canteen or a café or restaurant. You might think that this would encourage gluttony, but in France restaurants are not judged purely on the quantity of food per portion. And even if French people do take two hours for lunch (which is, honestly, not often the case on workdays), they will spend half the time talking rather than eating. Coffee alone will take twenty minutes.

Of course, lots of people don't have time for a full sit-down meal. If a company doesn't have a canteen, it is usually obliged to give lunch vouchers – *tickets restaurant* – and these will often be exchanged at the nearest *boulangerie*. Even here, amidst the chocolate cakes and buttery tarts, healthy eating is high on the menu. A cheese or ham sandwich will probably be *aux crudités* – with lettuce and tomato – and will have one slice of cheese rather than the four that are stuffed into an American sandwich. *Boulangeries* frequently do punnets of salad, too. The average lunch voucher will buy a sandwich, a cake and a drink. And half the customers will take mineral water as the drink.

So yes, like all the developed nations, the French are getting fatter. But they are doing so less quickly, because most of them just aren't interested in eating processed garbage instead of balanced meals. Simple, really.

Lie Back and Think of France

This is not to say that the French don't go in for stomach-blastingly big meals. A family Sunday lunch can easily last from one o'clock till four. And if you're invited to dinner in some parts of France – Auvergne, say, where the food is rich and fatty, based on pork and creamy cheeses – you'll have to be rolled home afterwards in a wheelbarrow.

I was once invited to the launch of a cookbook by a Parisian chef. He sat ten of us down to the biggest lunch I've ever eaten. Some of the dishes we ate have been erased from my memory (though probably not from my liver) but I do remember a thick steak of seared tuna, a slice of grilled *foie gras*, a pan-fried *magret de canard* (fillet of duck), truffle risotto, a dessert involving fresh rasp-berries, slices of dark chocolate and real gold leaf, a billiard-table-sized cheese trolley and lots of aperitify nibbles and coffee cakes. All this plus at least three sorts of wine and a tongue-burning *digestif*. I didn't try everything because I don't eat meat, but even so I had to go and lie down for what was left of the daylight to digest it all. And I – like most of the other guests, I expect – skipped dinner and the following day's break-fast and lunch to recover.

The French have a word for this Epicureanism that can't be translated into English – *gourmandise*. Some dictionaries have it as 'gluttony', but that's wrong, because gluttony is a negative thing, whereas *gourmandise* is a healthily sensual desire for the taste and texture of food. A *gourmandise* is another word for a treat, and the word can also be applied to sexual appetite.

The French sometimes overindulge their *gourmandise* and get a bout of severe indigestion, but if they do, they call it a *crise de foie*, a 'liver crisis'. It's not their fault, they haven't really eaten too much, it's just that their liver is having a bit of a nervous breakdown.

Half-boiled Notions

The very opposite of this gastronomic ideal is, in the minds of the French, English food. They will swear that the Brits spend their lives chewing mournfully on boiled beef, overcooked swede and plastic cheese, all washed down with lashings of warm, flat beer.

Just after I first arrived in France, I invited a French couple to a 'typically English' dinner. As an aperitif, I served weak tea with the tiniest smudge of milk. It looked like a sample of the River Thames. The main course was half-boiled, unpeeled potatoes garnished with a spoonful of raspberry jam. I told them that a joint of lamb had been bubbling in salt water all day, and was just a few minutes away from being properly boiled through.

They sipped politely at the tea, and the woman even tried a bit of potato, though her boyfriend was already looking at me as if to say, OK, I surrender, let's go to the restaurant now. The thing was, they weren't completely sure it was a joke, and were trying to find a polite way of asking. I eventually owned up to prevent the woman from having to eat a second hunk of dirty, uncooked spud, and said now I was going to serve the real English food – a vegetable curry.

Which they loved, by the way. The French will eat anything with flavour.

There are lots of British foods that the French adore – cakes, biscuits, Earl Grey, Stilton, fried bacon rashers, and even our thin, triangular sandwiches. I used to work near a Monoprix supermarket in Paris, and was astonished to see that their sandwiches were imported daily from an industrial estate in the Midlands.

However, one thing the French complain about a lot is the quality of food in trendy British restaurants. I agree with them. I've been to too many places in the UK that have obviously spent millions on décor, recruited their staff from modelling agencies and hired the poet laureate to write their menus, but fill their designer plates with microwaved trash.

In France, you can usually be sure that even the trendiest eatery will have invested more in the food than it has in the light fittings.

The French have a similar double-edged relationship with American food. It's all junk, they will say – sugar-filled, genetically modified, mass-produced, over-packaged and tasteless. They even use the English term *le fast-food* to distinguish it from anything French (although the dictionaries suggest that they ought to be saying *la restauration rapide*). Despite this, half of France's teenagers flock to eat *le fast-food* after school, and whole families chow down on cheap hamburgers as a treat in the middle of their Saturday shopping expedition.

The French may eat a lot of healthy food, but they enjoy the odd fatty, ketchupy binge as much as anyone. And secretly most French people have the occasional fantasy about being American. A quick, guilty chomp on a hamburger makes them feel as though they're driving along Route 66, rapping on a New York street corner or having sex with the cast of *Friends*.

A Better Class of Alcoholic

The French have a reputation as a nation of boozers. They will defend themselves by saying that at least their alcoholics do it in style. As the French yachtsman Olivier de Kersauson put it: 'I'm amazed that the police carry out breath tests to find out how much alcohol people have in their blood without testing for the vintage.'[18]

According to the French medical institute Inserm, there are over twenty thousand alcohol-related deaths per year in France. And this is not counting accidents while under the influence. For a similar population, the UK records only around six thousand deaths.

Even so, the French do generally go in for a more civilized style of drinking than most 'Anglo-Saxons', and they always have done. Apparently back in the eleventh century, William the Conqueror's invading Normans were shocked by the Saxons' habit of deliberately setting

[18] This, by the way, was the sailor who once claimed to have been slowed down during a round-the-world race by a sixty-foot squid clamped to the hull of his boat.

out to get paralytic. Things haven't changed much since. You will never hear a Frenchman say, 'OK, let's go and get pissed' (or its French equivalent) on a Friday night. They do get drunk, but it's usually because of heavy consumption during a meal or at a party. Getting sozzled is a by-product of their evening rather than its *raison d'être*.

This is why there are so many drink-driving deaths – around 40 per cent of French road fatalities are caused by alcohol. At the end of an evening, after a *bon dîner* accompanied by plenty of *bon vin*, a respectable middle-class driver will have a quick coffee 'to clear his head' and then go and smash his car into an oncoming bus; the theory being that after a good bottle of Château Margaux you can't possibly be as drunk as some vulgar English beer-drinker.

What's more, a driver who isn't yet completely sozzled can drop into virtually any service station and buy alcohol. The French don't seem to have cottoned on to the possible correlation between selling booze at service stations and drink-driving.

The problem is made worse because French clubbers do not go in for electing one of their number as a tee-totaller for the night when they drive to out-of-town discos. Every Friday and Saturday, after a long night of clubbing, carloads of young revellers end their short lives squashed against one of the plane trees that line French provincial roads.

With typical French logic, some regions are trying to tackle this drink-driving problem by (you guessed it) chopping down the plane trees.

Support the Save the Cheese Fund

Charles de Gaulle once said, 'How can you govern a country that produces 258 sorts of cheese?' The answer is pretty obvious – you simply dole out 258 sorts of cheese subsidies. And sausage subsidies, olive subsidies, wine subsidies, etc, etc.

It may seem slightly unfair to be paying 40 per cent of the European Union's budget in subsidies to 2 per cent of the population – the farmers – but the French say that this is necessary to preserve their traditional foods. Which is partly true. Without subsidies, the local producers of cheese so rustic you can see the farmer's fingerprints on the skin would be swamped by a tide of multinational, clingfilm-wrapped pseudo-Cheddar.

But it would be a mistake to think that these French food producers are all crusty peasants eking out a meagre living on a one-room, one-donkey farmstead. Apart from the fact that France has its own multinational food companies, some of the old *paysans* I've met are as deft with their finances as the best Wall Street trader.

I was once shown around a farm in central France belonging to an old couple who dressed as if they needed clothes subsidies. A barn-shaped nylon dress for her, medieval blue dungarees and a scarecrow shirt for him. They showed me their open chicken run populated by a few scrawny hens, and their three fields, all of them empty apart from four or five bright-orange cows (naturally orange, I should add – they were Limousines). An old Renault was parked in what used to be a chestnut-drying shed.[19] You would have thought that they were heading for starvation within the next few months.

But no, not at all. The friend who'd taken me to the farm explained that the old couple, like all their friends and families on similar farms, were very comfortably off. They got European subsidies every year for planting new apple trees, a payment for burning most of the crop and so countering over-production, then a subsidy for ripping out the trees and reducing the national apple-growing capacity. They were also buying up fields all around the village and applying for more grants for leaving them fallow. Starvation was a very, very long way away. In Brussels, perhaps.

Given that any attempt by the French government to reduce subsidies causes blocked motorways and heaps of rotting food dumped outside (and sometimes inside) government offices, it will be difficult to take any of these advantages away from the farmers.

In any case, food is very important to French politicians. President Chirac has been accused of several cases of fraud. Not for simply filling his pockets, though. He was indicted because of his vast *frais de bouche* ('mouth expenses') when he was mayor of Paris. It was alleged that he spent 2.13 million euros of city funds on food between 1987 and 1995 – excluding official receptions. That is 4,500

. . . .

[19] The cows have nothing in common with the luxury cars except their name. Apparently limos are so named because the first cars with an enclosed section for passengers had roofs shaped like the hoods of cloaks worn in Limousin, not because they looked or drove like cows.

euros a week on private meals for his wife and himself. The investigating magistrate threw the case out, so apparently this is a perfectly acceptable sum to spend on food.

Another accusation concerned using state funds to fly Madame Chirac to attend the making of the world's biggest mushroom omelette in the city of Brive in 1998. Surely only a French politician would risk discrediting his administration for an omelette.

Food Laws and Rituals

Because the French spend so many hours of their lives at the lunch and dinner table, they are sticklers for food etiquette, and have been for a long time. It was Cardinal Richelieu who introduced the round-tipped knife to European tables in 1669 after he declared that it was vulgar for gentlemen to pick their teeth with their knife points at the end of a meal.

Some of the rules listed below may seem very sexist, but France is still that kind of a place. I once started a job in Paris on the day of the firm's Christmas party. My boss, a woman, nominated me, as one of the few men there, to open the champagne. She quickly regretted it when I let the cork fly out of the bottle. It bounced off the ceiling and hit her on the head. I and most of the other staff laughed, and it took her three months to start paying my salary.

Here are some more present-day food rituals that must be followed in *la bonne société*:

- At table, diners must always be seated man-woman-man-woman. This rule must be adhered to even if some guests are gay.

- At the restaurant, women order first.

- At table, there should always be glasses for wine and water. The water glasses should be bigger than the wine glasses. The wine glasses will probably be filled more often, but at least a token gesture towards sobriety has been made.

- Non-French wine should be ordered only in an ethnic restaurant or if all bottles of French wine in the restaurant have been smashed and/or drunk by visiting rugby fans.

- At a restaurant, waiters will ask who is going to taste the wine. Men usually do so.

- At home, the first few drops of a new bottle of wine should be poured into one's own glass (in case there are any cork remnants). After that, women's glasses are filled first, then men's.

- When opening champagne, hold the cork and turn the bottle. Don't let the cork go, and don't try to *sabrer le champagne* (cut the top of the bottle off with a sabre blow) unless you are a fencing expert, otherwise the room will be full of champagne spray and flying glass.

- Before touching your food, it is polite to say 'Bon *appétit.*' And men should not start eating until the women have taken their first forkful.

- It is polite to discuss food at the table, but not (for too long, anyway) what you are actually eating. At the restaurant you should, however, ask your fellow diners what their food is like.

- There is a new fad in Paris that involves eating using only a fork that you hold like a pen or a chopstick. Obviously it doesn't work if you've got a hunk of meat on your plate, but when eating anything lighter, like a salad or a plate of vegetables, it seems to be considered more refined to leave your knife on the table. When using the knife to cut meat, some French people hold the fork vertically like a skewer. Parisians think this is vulgar and (even worse) provincial.

- Knives should never be crossed – on the table, on worktops or in the sink waiting to be washed. This symbolizes conflict (probably about who's going to do the washing-up).

- Meat may be served when almost raw (or in the case of *steak tartare*, totally raw). It will cause offence to send bloody, red-centred roast beef back to the chef saying it is uncooked. So remember the different stages of cooking when you are asked '*Quelle cuisson?*' ('How would you like it cooked?') From raw to well done, they are: *bleu*, *saignant* ('bloody'), *à point* and *bien cuit*. If you want it cooked all the way through, it might be best to say '*Très bien cuit, s'il vous plaît.*' Some waiters might cheekily add an *à l'américaine* option, meaning as hard as a cowboy's boot sole.

- Salad without dressing is not salad, it is a pile of ingredients. Even grated carrot needs at the very least a few drops of lemon juice. It is usual to make the dressing in the salad bowl, then tip the salad loosely on top. Don't toss the salad until the last minute or it will go soggy.

- Never cut lettuce on your plate. This is because, long ago, when cutlery was made of iron, the vinaigrette made the lettuce taste of metal.

- Obviously you never cut oysters or mussels. Oysters should be loosened from the shell using the little fork provided, then slurped down whole. Mussels should be picked out of the shell using a mussel shell as tweezers. The French have no qualms about eating shellfish with their fingers. Seafood platters involve hours of tearing, twisting, picking and snapping, and that's what the finger bowls (*rince-doigts*) or (in less chic places) towelettes in a sachet are for.

- Only eat shellfish in months that contain an 'r'. This rules out the summer months when the sea is relatively warm and storage difficult. Most people ignore the rule when they're eating by the sea, but eating oysters in Paris in August is for tourists with lead-lined digestive tracts.

- Never put a loaf of bread upside-down on the table. This is bad luck.

- If you want to wipe your plate (there is a verb for this – *saucer*, pronounced 'sossay'), then use a piece of bread skewered on the end of your fork. It is not really the done thing to push the bread around the plate with your fingers, though people do it.

- Similarly, you are not supposed to dunk croissants or *tartines* (buttered bread) into your coffee at breakfast, but it seems a crime not to. No one will look askance if you do this in a café.

- When having a cheese fondue, don't drop your bread into the saucepan. Anyone doing this will have to do a forfeit (*gage*), such as hopping around the table three times or (worse) doing all the washing-up.

Finally a couple of rules that are less about etiquette than about understanding the food put in front of you:

- Remember that a small furry animal is not cute – it is a meal in waiting. Comments like 'poor little bunny' will only provoke laughter and/or scorn.

- Just because something smells like poo does not mean it will taste like it. Reblochon cheese, for example, can smell faintly (or not so faintly) of a urine-soaked sock. But grilled over a dish of potatoes it is sublime. If you are served a particularly ripe-smelling cheese or sausage, breathe through the mouth and take a bite. You might well get a pleasant surprise. If you get an unpleasant surprise, remember that in France, one spits to the right.

Mouton Dressed as Lamb

The French have few scruples about calling a spade a spade, or a brain a brain, when they're talking about food. For a start, in French *porc*, *boeuf*, *mouton* and *veau* (calf/veal) are the names of the animals, so when talking about the relevant meat, the actual furry four-legged creature automatically springs to mind (as it does with lamb in English, of course). This, coupled with their taste for unusual parts of the animal, can produce some graphic-sounding translations.

French food that would sound unappetizing, or just plain silly, if it had an English name

Back of pig's knee	*jarret de porc*	
Bastard	*bâtard*	large baguette
Blurred eggs	*oeufs brouillés*	scrambled eggs
Blown-out cheese	*soufflé au fromage*	
Bull's cheek	*joue de boeuf*	
Calf's thyroid	*ris de veau*	
Chocolate lightning	*éclair au chocolat*	
Cock with wine	*coq au vin*	
Fat liver	*foie gras*	
Gob-amuser	*amuse-gueule*	aperitif nibble
Guts	*tripes*	
Little lamb's rib	*côtelette d'agneau*	
Little ovens	*petits fours*	
Lost bread	*pain perdu*	bread pudding
Nun's fart	*pet de nonne*	small doughnut
Part of the butcher	*pièce du boucher*	prime cut of meat
Pig's foot	*pied de porc*	
Rawnesses	*crudités*	
Rust	*rouille*	sauce eaten with fish soup

A French invention that was not adopted by the rest of the world, the long-distance suppository applicator.

THE
4TH
COMMANDMENT

Tu Seras Malade
THOU SHALT BE ILL

THOU SHALT BE ILL

IN 1673, FRANCE'S GREATEST COMIC DRAMATIST, MOLIÈRE, wrote a play called Le Malade Imaginaire – The Hypochondriac – about a man who is so obsessed with his health problems that he wants to marry his daughter to a doctor to save on medical bills, and threatens to banish her to a convent if she refuses. It was supposed to be a satire, but the French seem to have decided that he is a role model rather than an anti-hero.

In this they are aided and abetted by the state. The French social-security system may be cutting back on expenses, but it is still one of the most generous in the world, and this encourages the French to get ill as often as possible.

It's always surprising to go to a pharmacy in a seaside resort in midsummer and see masses of people there. And they're not just buying sun cream, condoms and insect repellent. It's as if on holiday they have time to realize how ill they really are and decide to try out all the remedies. And although the French have been saying for at least the last decade that their health service is about to collapse, it keeps going strong. Partly because the government commits so much money to its public services, but also because there is cash in the system. Patients pay out and are then reimbursed. This cash pays doctors and pharmacists, and keeps things turning over.

At first, it can feel strange to give your doctor a cheque at the end of your appointment, but the discomfort is relieved when 70 per cent of the price is refunded by the social security. And if you work and have a good *mutuelle* (private health top-up scheme), the refund can be 100 per cent of your costs, even for things like capped teeth and glasses.

Even so, the French aren't satisfied.[20]

The best example of this dissatisfaction I ever heard was at a spa hotel in the southwest of France. I had come for a long weekend of relaxing massages and seaweed baths, and was surprised to discover that before they would let me anywhere near the hot tubs, I had to see a doctor, who was going to prescribe my treatments. 'Don't worry,' I was told, *'la visite est remboursée'* – the consultation would be refunded by the state. I seriously considered asking whether the same applied to the minibar.

As I sat in the waiting room in my fluffy bathrobe, I listened to two elderly ladies discussing the French health system. It was 'going to the devil', they agreed. I thought they were repeating the common complaint about *le trou de la sécu* – the 'hole in the social-security system' or health-budget deficit. Most years, France overspends on

----

[20] Because they never are.

health by several billion euros. Not surprising, really, if all the French guests at this spa spent twenty euros or so of the state's money to see a doctor when all they wanted was a bubble bath.

But no, this wasn't what was bothering the two ladies. It was the difficulty one of them had had persuading her doctor to prescribe the spa treatment itself as a medical necessity. She'd been going on *cures* for twenty years, she said, and it had always been automatic before. This time, the doctor had forced her to identify some specific problem (she'd chosen sciatica) to treat, rather than prescribing her a week of massages and sploshing about in a seawater swimming pool just for her general well-being. Soon, she said, they might be limited to the purely medical spas like Aix les Bains – a former Roman spa in the Alps, famed for its sulphurous waters and casinos.

I had to admit that the situation was getting drastic.

My *visite médicale* was a farce. The doctor weighed me, checked that I still had a spine, asked if I was averse to being stood against a wall and sprayed with a high-power hose of cold water (er, yes), and ticked a few treatments on the spa's menu.

I saw that he had ticked two sessions of aquagym, which sounded a bit strenuous.

'Can't I exchange those for seaweed bubble baths?' I asked.

'OK, if you prefer,' he said, and made the change. My highly scientific medical prescription was complete.

While I was simmering away in my fishy-smelling tub, I tried to calculate what all this was costing. If the spa had, say, a hundred guests a week for fifty weeks of the year, and all of them paid twenty euros to see the doctor, that came to a hundred thousand euros a year. The state refunds only 70 per cent of medical expenses for most adults, but even so that was a hefty sum, just at this one spa. And if only a tenth of the elderly guests got their whole treatment paid for, you could probably double the cost to the state. If you added on the national-insurance cover paid by the state for the spa's employees…my mental arithmetic fizzled out as I did a typical French shrug (very easy to perform when you're lounging in a vast bathtub) and decided it wasn't my problem. I had no complaints about the French health service at all.

Big Boobs

The government has taken some steps to reduce health spending by encouraging the use of generic drugs and cutting the list of refundable medicines. But no government would dare to get too tough on health for fear of losing the next election and/or provoking mass demonstrations.

So as not to appear totally inactive, the health minister announced a crackdown on medical fraud. Some of the examples of health cheating quoted in the press were very revealing.

One woman had been going to see various doctors seventy-five times a month, and getting prescriptions for an average of twelve boxes of antidepressants per day. Another woman had tricked a doctor into prescribing a breast enlargement after claiming that her boobs had shrunk after an accident. But these frauds are only cases of people pushing back the boundaries of what is legally, acceptably available on the national health. It is perfectly acceptable for a woman to have a breast enhancement paid for by the state if her boobs are not symmetrical enough to be shown off on a French beach.

And France is only now, and very slowly, introducing a scheme which will force people to register with a single general practitioner. In the past, people could have several GPs if they wanted, and visit whichever of them could offer an appointment at the most convenient time. Also, because doctors are paid per consultation, they can be tempted to outdo one another in generosity in an attempt to hold on to their fickle patients.

A friend of mine, who had just qualified as a doctor, went to do a holiday replacement for a GP in a large Breton town. On her first day, a man came and told her he was having recurring headaches and needed a CAT scan to make sure he didn't have a brain tumour. My friend said that it might be better to examine him, discuss possible causes and maybe do some other tests first.

'Docteur X' (the woman my friend was replacing) 'prescribed one for me last month,' the man said

'You had a CAT scan last month? Do you have the results with you?' my friend asked.

The man lost his temper, and said he was going to visit Docteur Y, who had a reputation for knowing how to look after his patients properly. He stormed off to get his prescription for a repeat brain scan elsewhere.

This is an extreme example, but my friend said that lots of the patients she saw came with a shopping list of (frequently very expensive) drugs that the regular doctor always gave them without putting up any resistance. The doctor's surgery was just a stop on the way to the pharmacy.

Getting the Green Light

This national drug habit explains why France looks so brightly lit when seen from outer space. Its towns are decorated with green neon crosses indicating the presence of a pharmacy. I live in the centre of Paris, and there are three large pharmacies within two hundred yards of my house. They are not English- or American-style drug stores, boosting their income by selling food, toys and cheap shampoo. These are fully medicalized pharmacies, surviving (very comfortably) by filling prescriptions and selling over-the-counter medicine, as well as certain pharmacy-only brands of beauty treatment and health supplements.

The pharmacies have a total monopoly on the sale of anything at all medical. I recently had a chronic toothache while away for a weekend in Normandy. It kept me awake all Saturday night, all the more so because of my annoyance when I found that I'd forgotten to bring any aspirin with me. On the Sunday morning, I went to the local pharmacy, but it was closed. I tried all the shops in the town, but none of them could sell me aspirin, paraceta-mol or any painkiller other than alcohol. Only the pharmacy was allowed to sell them. The address of the *pharmacie de garde* (duty pharmacy) would be written on the door, the café barman told me.

There was no address, just a phone number to call to find out where the nearest duty pharmacy was. It was 18, the emergency services number.

I phoned, apologized profusely for bothering them with my trivial problem, and was told that the nearest open pharmacy was twenty kilometres away. As I didn't have a car, it was going to cost me a return taxi ride just to buy a box of aspirin. I was tempted to ask for an ambulance. It might well have worked.

All this because the pharmacists' lobby is so strong in France that even the lowest grade of non-prescription medicine can only be bought in a pharmacy. So if you live outside a big town, you just have to wait till Monday.

In the end, I decided to conduct a door-to-door search at the hotel, and the first person who answered had a toilet bag stuffed with the full hypochondriac's selection of cures for everything from headaches to cholera, and gave me enough painkillers to tide me over till the Monday.

And on the Monday, I went to see my wonderful, fully refundable, state-system dentist, whose surgery is straight out of a sci-fi movie. There are some things it's hard to complain about.

Special Treatment

Despite new restrictions as to which specialists the French can go and see without a referral from their family doctor, it is still very quick and easy to get an appointment with people who would be kept hidden behind walls of bureaucracy in Britain.

Women go directly to a gynaecologist for the Pill or a check-up, and children can have specialist paediatricians as their regular doctors. Outside a hospital like the Hôtel Dieu in Paris, the specialists are listed on a noticeboard, with the telephone number of their surgery. If a GP prescribes a visit to any of the specialists at a hospital, the appointment will often be given within days.

This does have a downside. I once had a sinus problem, and a friend recommended a *'merveilleux'* ear, nose and throat man. I went along to his surgery, a posh apartment in the west of Paris, and walked into a modern art gallery. A car salesman in a flash suit arrived, took me into his designer-catalogue office, tapped around on my face with his gold-laden fingers, and asked me whether I was free for the operation at his clinic two days later.

He misinterpreted my shocked silence. 'It's all refundable,' he said.

I said I'd think about it, and he gave me an insurance man's business card and told me to call him as soon as I'd made my mind up. In the end, I took the English way out, bought a nasal spray, and saved the French state thousands of euros. They really ought to offer me a sea-water spa weekend to thank me.

Vive la Différence

The differences between what you can expect from the British and French national-health services in the case of various common ailments:

A COLD

FRANCE: Call your doctor, get an appointment for the next day, or maybe even the same day. Go to a small private-looking apartment, and wait in what looks like a living room with an abnormally large number of magazines on the coffee table. Look at the fashion pages of a recent *Elle* or news magazine. Be welcomed personally by the doctor, who comes to fetch you, probably just a few minutes late if he or she is not an especially popular or inefficient practician. Explain your problem, have your throat examined, your ganglions felt, your temperature taken with a thermometer pressed on the forehead or in the ear (the days of the rectal probe are gone, much to the chagrin of some). Listen while your doctor tells you the Greek names for sore throat and runny nose (which all the French know). Watch him or her write out a prescription for aspirin, throat pastilles, nasal spray, chest rub, tablets for a steam inhalant, antibiotics in case things get worse, and (probably only on request these days) suppositories. Ask for, and receive, a three-day sick note. Pay the doctor by cheque, and leave the surgery, shaking the doctor's hand, promising to return if the cold doesn't clear up in the next few days.

Go to a pharmacy, get a rucksack full of medicine,

watch the pharmacist swipe your social-security card[21] so that your refund is credited automatically. Go home, have an aspirin and a hot drink and wait for the cold virus to go away naturally. In the case of recurring snuffles, request a stay at Aix les Bains health spa.

BRITAIN: Call the doctor's surgery, be told that there are no appointments free for the next week and to call back in forty-eight hours if you're not cured or dead. Go to the supermarket, buy a medicated drink, go to work and sneeze all over workmates. In the case of recurring snuffles, try acupuncture.

BACKACHE

FRANCE: Two choices. One: go to an osteopathic doctor, who will give one very costly session of treatment that will be refunded by the state because it counts as a diagnosis. In some cases this will cure the problem. Two: go to the doctor and request a course of physiotherapy. Get a prescription for twenty sessions. Find a physiotherapist, go to his or her apartment once or twice a week for massage and exercises, pay (an admittedly large sum) at the end of the twenty sessions and wait for the refund to be paid into your bank account. If the problem is more serious and requires an operation, it will be performed within a month, either at a state hospital or a private clinic. In both cases, most of the cost will be refunded by the state.

....

[21] This is known as the *carte vitale*, or lifesaving card, showing how central the health service is in the national psyche.

BRITAIN: Two choices. One: after finally getting an appointment with the doctor, listen to him or her prescribe rest and painkillers and, if the problem persists, make a return visit to arrange a one-off session with a physiotherapist at the local hospital who might be free in six months. Two: find your own physiotherapist, osteopath or acupuncturist, who may or may not be qualified. Spend a fortune and hope for the best.

OLD AGE

FRANCE: Visit several doctors (all of them refundable), have a nice chat, get prescriptions for hormone-replacement pills, the latest anti-rheumatism and anti-arthritis drugs, sleeping tablets, food supplements and two weeks at a spa (all of them refundable). Go to the electricity, gas and water companies to confirm with them that it is illegal to switch off your supply even if you never pay the bill. Inform your landlord that it is illegal to evict you or increase your rent, even if your lease is up and the market value of the property means that it would not be excessive to double your rent.

BRITAIN: Put on all your woollies and have a nice cup of tea. Or move to France.

Phrases you might need when going to see a French doctor

J'ai une rhino-pharyngite/une otite.	*Djay oon reeno-faran-djeet/ oon oh-teet.*	I have a bit of a head cold/an earache.

(French translations for very minor illnesses are often impressively Greek.)

Est-ce que j'ai vraiment besoin de tous ces médicaments?	*Ess-ka djay vray-mo be-zwa de too say may-dee-ka-mo?*	Do I really need all these drugs?
Est-ce que c'est remboursé?	*Ess-ka say rom-bor-say?*	Will it be refunded?
Pouvez-vous me donner une ordonnance pour une radio?	*Poovay voo me donnay oon ordononce por oon rah dyo?*	Can you prescribe me an X-ray? (*Radio* is short for *radiographie*.)
Je peux voir quels spécialistes sans ordonnance?	*Dje peu vwar kel spessy aleest sonz ordononce?*	Which specialists can I visit without a referral?
Est-ce que je pourrais avoir une ordonnance pour une cure?	*Ess-ka dje pooray a-vwa roon ordononce por oon kur?*	Can I have a prescription for a spa cure?

CONTINUED...

Je n'ai jamais utilisé de suppositoire. Comment on fait?	*Dje nay djamay ootee leezay de soopozitwar. Komo o'fay?*	I've never used a suppository. What do I do with it?
Insérez fermement dans l'anus et serrez fort.	*Ansayray fair m'mon don lannoose ay serray for.*	Insert firmly into your back passage and clench.

JACQUES: *'Voulez-vous coucher avec moi ce soir?'*
LIZ: *'One is not amused.'*
Monsieur Chirac's refusal to speak English earns him a right royal brush-off.

THE
5TH
COMMANDMENT

Tu Parleras Français
THOU SHALT SPEAK FRENCH

THOU SHALT SPEAK FRENCH

PRESIDENT JACQUES CHIRAC RECENTLY MADE A POINT OF disrupting a European Union summit because the proceedings were being held in English rather than French. What annoyed him was that the man making the speech was French – Ernest-Antoine Seillière, the leader of the European business lobby UNICE. When Chirac interrupted to ask why he wasn't speaking in French, Seillière replied, 'Because the language of business is English.' This was one truth too far, and the president and three of his ministers stormed out.[22]

Yes, French bitterness about the way some of their inventions are ignored is very similar to the feeling they have that the planet has been robbed of its rightful world language – French. France still thinks that the

....

[22] What annoyed Chirac more was that the subject of the debate was French protectionism. With sublime French irony, diplomats later explained the walkout by saying that the president and his ministers all needed a toilet break. This was probably a French in-joke – their favourite phrase for 'you're annoying me' is *tu me fais chier* or 'you make me shit'.

world would be a much more diplomatic place if debates at the EU and the UN were held in French. They forget that ambassadors would spend all their time nit-picking about subjunctive verb forms, and countries would get invaded because no one could agree on the adjectival endings in the peace accord.[23]

And this is not the only reason why having French as a world language would be totally unbearable. The other is a political gaffe that the French can't help committing. How can they expect other countries to use French as a national language when they mercilessly take the pee out of anyone that tries? The French make jokes about the accents of French-speaking Belgians, Swiss, Canadians, Tahitians, New Caledonians, Caribbean Islanders and Africans. French TV often subtitles anyone with a non-standard accent, as if their way of speaking is so yokelish that no civilized viewer will understand.

All this goes to explain a certain ambiguity that some French people feel when a foreigner tries to speak the language. They are happy that someone has been (temporarily, at least) converted to the belief that French must be spoken. And they are glad that they can be superior to you, because they know when you make a mistake.

However, they do feel genuine pleasure when you get French right. I started to get invited on to French radio

----

[23] In the seventeenth and eighteenth centuries, French was the international language of diplomacy, a period during which all the major European powers were almost constantly at war.

and TV a lot as soon as producers found out that I could speak good French. Their reasoning was obvious. It doesn't make good listening if a guest is jabbering incomprehensibly (except on certain reality TV shows, of course). But I only started getting invited back on to the same shows when they realized that I could actually make jokes without getting the grammar wrong. That was *très raffiné*.

Which reminds me – there's a French joke that is funny only because the grammar in the punchline is correct. Just so you get it, let me explain in advance that the penultimate word, 'fût', is the imperfect subjunctive of the verb 'to be' (the imperfect subjunctive being a rarely used and rather pompous tense).

Here's the joke, in English first for those who don't speak good enough French to enjoy the full impact of an imperfect subjunctive:

A Frenchman is talking to a Scot.

'Have you ever tried haggis?' the Scot asks.

'Yes,' the Frenchman replies.

'What did you think?' the Scot asks.

'At first I thought it was shit. Then I regretted that it wasn't.'

The punchline in French goes like this:

'D'abord j'ai cru que c'était de la merde. Ensuite, j'ai regretté que ça n'en fût pas.'

Hilarious, right?

Yes, hilariously right.

Parlez-vous Right?

Worse than the fact that few nations in the world can be bothered to argue about sanctions and wars in French is the deep-seated fear that their language is being killed off by English. This idea is, of course, totally ridiculous. Even French teenagers who listen to radio ads exhorting them to go 'on line et chat avec tes friends' are incapable of stringing an English sentence together. And when they go on line, they use a uniquely French chat-speak in which *'qu'est-ce que tu fais'* becomes *'kes tu fé'*.

What the French-language protectionists are scared of is exactly what is annoying grammarians and historians of every language in the world – the language is alive and changing, and there's nothing the grammar control freaks can do about it.

But the French, more than most other people, still love centralized control of every aspect of life. Which is why the protectionists are so adamant that the French language must not change unless they say so. Each new word admitted into the language does not officially exist until it has been vetted and okayed by the Académie Française and its team of forty modestly named *immortels*. And whereas English-dictionary compilers happily list any foreign word they pick up, from coulis to karaoke via fromage frais, the *immortels* usually try to veto foreign expressions and impose French words in their place.

Well-known examples have included the ridiculous attempt in the 1980s to get French business-school tutors to use *mercatique* instead of marketing, the partially successful campaign to impose *baladeur* instead of Walkman, and the ridiculously literal *gomme à mâcher* that failed to replace chewing gum (or 'shwing-gom', as the French pronounce it).

The English-haters have recently tried to get the French to write *courriels* instead of emails, and when that didn't work, in a fit of desperation they gallicized the spelling of 'mail' to *mel*. To no avail – the French usually talk about sending each other *un mail*.

The tragedy for the *immortels* is that the French – like everyone else – only use dictionaries to look up words they don't understand, and they understand the anglicisms because they hear them all the time. So banning them from the dictionary makes no difference at all.[24]

Ordinary French mortals love using – and abusing – English words. To be trendy, they'll talk about *mon boyfriend* and they'll say that something classy is *trop style* (pronouncing *'style' à l'anglaise* – 'tro stile'). Sometimes they get English words totally wrong. For example, instead of saying something is hip, they say it's *hype* (to rhyme with 'stripe'). And they abbreviate *bon weekend* (have a good weekend) to the absurd misnomer *bon week*.

They also invent their own English words that aren't English at all. Everyone knows about *le camping* (campsite), *le parking* (car park), *le living* (living room), *le shampooing*

....

[24] In fact, new words, many of them of English origin, are added to each year's new edition of the *Petit Larousse* dictionary. But this is mainly to infuriate the Académie and use the resulting media coverage to sell more books.

(shampoo – pronounced 'shom-pwang') and *le footing* (an old word for jogging). And for the last few years they've been using *le fooding* when they talk about going to *hype* restaurants. L*e fooding*? It's enough to put you off your dinner.

But all this linguistic frolicking is a leisure pursuit. Deliberately using English words is fun because they know it's naughty. They're kicking against *l'establishment*. When it comes down to the serious matter of writing French, most people are sticklers for getting things right. Grammatical mistakes on the page are not *style* at all.

These Boots Were Made for Talking

It would be a grave mistake to underestimate the importance of grammar. Grammar, along with spelling, can be simply right or wrong, so it is incredibly important to the French. Spelling is an integral part of French grammar because the verbs are so difficult to conjugate, and because lots of grammatically different words sound alike. Four verb endings *–ai*, *–ais*, *–ait* and *–aient* all sound exactly the same. And the practically indistinguishable *verre* (glass), *vers* (verse or towards), *ver* (worm), and *vert* (green) give French kids nightmares. Or their teachers, anyway.[25]

. . . .

[25] The same goes for the identically pronounced *vin* (wine), *vain* (vain), *vingt* (twenty) and *vint* (came), and *saut* (jump), *seau* (bucket), *sot* (idiot) and *sceau* (wax seal), to give just two common examples.

The French are proud that their grammar is so complicated that even they don't understand it. Just ask a group of three well-educated French people to translate the phrase 'I love the shoes you gave me.' If they don't think too hard, at least one of them will make a grammatical mistake when writing out the sentence in French. If they do think about it, they'll be able to argue for hours and will end up digging around for the grammar book they had at school and have never thrown away so that they can prove their point.[26] And if you know the rules and can get sentences like this right, or even if you simply realize that there is a difficulty here and can take part in the discussion, they'll love you.

But back to the shoes.

The two main contenders for grammatical rightness will be: '*J'adore les chaussures que tu m'as offert*' and '*J'adore les chaussures que tu m'as offertes.*' But someone is bound to ask who's speaking here, and suggest that if it's a woman maybe it should be: '*J'adore les chaussures que tu m'as offerte.*'

So which is correct? It's '*J'adore les chaussures que tu m'as offertes.*'

If you really want to know why, by all means read the next paragraph, but be warned that it is complicated to the point of pointlessness. If you're not a grammar fetishist, I'd strongly advise moving on to the next section now.

. . . .

[26] In France, you can't throw away your school grammar book. It would be like taking the airbag out of your steering wheel. You never know when it might save your life.

Here goes: '*J'adore les chaussures que tu m'as offertes*' is correct because the past participle of the verb *offrir* (*offert*) is governed by the *que* which refers to the *chaussures* which are a direct object of the verb *offrir* and are feminine plural, so that *offert* needs the feminine 'e' and the plural 's'.

You see, it's simple when you know how.

It's even simpler to say just '*J'adore ces chaussures.*'

Who Are Vous?

The eternal problem – *tu* or *vous*? *Tutoyer* or *vouvoyer*, as they call it. Other languages have these familiar and unfamiliar forms, but in France people still use them as weapons.

Jean Cocteau summed up the snobbery that can be involved in making the wrong choice: 'I'm always prepared to call someone *tu*, as long as they don't call me *tu* in return,' he wrote in his diary. You almost wonder whether he called his diary *tu* or *vous*.

Tu is usually reserved for friends, lovers, family, animals, machines and anyone a French person considers inferior to themselves (which can cover a lot of people). During the riots of 2005, the Minister of the Interior criticized his police for calling all their suspects *tu*. [27]

....

[27] He was slower to reprimand some of them for arresting anyone with dark skin, but racial prejudice amongst the massively White-dominated French police seemed to be less important than the *tu/vous* protocol.

In the French translation of the Bible, everyone calls each other *tu*. Jesus and the disciples all *tutoyer* each other, as you would expect amongst a group of male friends. And God calls everyone *tu*, which is also pretty predictable given that He is superior to everyone else in creation.[28] It would be fun for someone to go through the Bible retranslating the dialogues into French, and deciding who really ought to show more respect and use *vous*. (Fun, in the totally neurotic, anally retentive sense of the word, that is.)

Getting your *tu* and *vous* right, though, is vital these days. Misusing *tu* can cause real offence, just as if someone said 'Hey, babe' to the Queen. I once saw the mayor of a large French town almost faint when a gauche foreign student at a city hall cocktail party asked him, 'Tu es qui, toi?' The student was merely asking the mayor in learner's French who he was, but ended up giving him a diplomatic kick in the testicles.

The student didn't realize what he was doing, but when *tu* is misused by a French person who understands fully what's going on, it can make you cringe. I have seen awkward interviews where a TV presenter gets too familiar, addresses a star as *tu* and receives a withering *vous* in reply. Because of this danger, even a none-too-chic teenage boy will address a girl in the street as *vous* before strategically changing to *tu* if his chat-up lines go

....

[28] That, incidentally, is why the commandments in this book are in the *tu* form. The originals were dictated to Moses by God, and passed on by Jesus, who addresses everyone, including Pontius Pilate, as if they were his friends and equals.

down well. TV panellists often address each other as *vous* on air, even though you know full well that they will be saying *tu* before and after the show. The *vouvoiement* gives the programme an air of polite stylishness.

In pretty well all workplaces, colleagues of equal rank call each other *tu*, but in a group conversation with their bosses, the intermingling of *tu* and *vous* can be dizzying. Even if you call your head of department or MD *tu*, your colleague who doesn't work with him or her as frequently might say *vous*. The boss might call everyone *tu* in a spirit of democracy, while simultaneously calling his secretary *vous* out of respect for a young subordinate. But while he calls his secretary *vous* during office hours, you know it's *tu* in private. *Oh oui*.

Lovers will almost always call each other *tu*, of course. They are on pretty familiar terms, after all. Though there is a class of bourgeois French couple that insists on calling each other *vous*. Whether they get an extra thrill by changing to *tu* in moments of great excitement is their own business.

Family gatherings can be just as complicated as company meetings. Most families call each other *tu*, from toddler to grandparent. Only a few bourgeois parents insist on *vous* from their children. However, even in the most laidback and welcoming of families, some people won't dare call their mothers- and fathers-in-law *tu*.

This whole problem can drive you crazy. Therefore, when in doubt, it is best to take the social weight off your feet by letting the French person decide. This can require a bit of linguistic dodging about. When you meet someone and you're not sure what to call them (or you might not remember whether you're on *tutoyer* terms, which is even more awkward), you have to act fast. The thing to do is get in with a '*Ça va?*' before they can, because the required reply is '*Oui, et toi/vous?*' If you get beaten to the draw, you can stay neutral by replying, '*Oui, très bien, merci, et ça va, le travail?*' ('How are things at work?') Other possibilities would be '*Ça va, la famille?*' (How's the family?), '*C'était bien, les vacances?*' ('How were your holidays?') or whatever you can think of asking them about without having to use *tu* or *vous*.

If you are really stuck, it is perfectly OK to say '*Oui, très bien merci, et vous?*' and add '*Ou est-ce qu'on se dit tu?*' – 'Or should we call each other *tu*?' The matter of how to address each other is an existential problem and is therefore a perfectly good subject for conversation.

Of course, if they reply '*Non, on se dit vous,*' you're in the *merde*.

When Are You an Idiot?

That question, '*Est-ce qu'on se dit tu?*', contains a potentially lethal trap in the obstacle course of French pronunciation. The extremely common construction *qu'on* is pronounced the same way as one of the worst insults in French, *con*.[29] Originally a slang word for the female

....

[29] For more on this and other swearwords, see the Tenth Commandment on politeness.

genitalia, it is now used to mean 'bloody stupid' or 'bloody idiot'.

The French are fairly lax about swearing, but even they can find it disturbing to insult people in the middle of half their sentences. This is why, in written and formal spoken French, people often change *qu'on* into the completely artificial *que l'on*.

The difficult French sound 'on' is said by pouting the lips and snorting the syllable through your nose. It is not to be confused with the very similar 'en', and 'an', which are more like an English 'on'. The danger comes if you mispronounce a word like *quand* (when) and end up saying *con*. This is especially tricky because it is not always obvious in a French tone of voice whether you're asking a question or making a statement. French questions don't go up at the end like English ones.

This combination of misunderstandings happened to an English friend of mine, who blew his chance of getting invited to a wedding on the Côte d'Azur in one short phone call. 'I'm getting married,' his French sort-of-friend told him. 'Oh yes, when?' the Brit wanted to inquire. Unfortunately, what he actually said was 'A*h oui*? C'*est con*' – 'Oh yes? That's bloody stupid.'

French is full of traps like this, especially if you're a foreigner and can't master the subtle differences between certain vowel sounds. One of the most difficult words to say in French is *surtout*, meaning 'especially', because it contains all three of the toughest sounds to pronounce. The short 'u', the long 'ou' and the guttural 'r'. Get them wrong and you can be in trouble.

For example, mispronounce *merci beaucoup* ('thanks very much') and you end up saying *merci beau cul*, or 'thanks, beautiful arse'. A mistake that can make you some interesting new acquaintances.

Similarly, a friend told me about a British accountant who came over from London head office to talk to her French colleagues and wanted to ask them about their high costs (*coûts*) but actually asked a meeting full of salesmen 'Why do you have such large arses?' (*culs*).

I once tried to inform a female colleague over the phone that I was just on my way to see her – *en route* – and later realized that I'd explained I was hurrying over *en rut* or 'on heat', like a rutting stag. When I walked into her office I wondered why she was holding her ruler baseball-bat-style. And if, like many Brits, you fail to pronounce your French 'r' gutturally enough at the end of *coeur*, you can make *cri de coeur* – a cry from the heart – sound exactly like *cri de queue*, a rather more vulgar cry from the prick. Although for French men that can often be more or less the same thing.

Another trap is the word *plein* or full. If you've had enough to eat, you can't say '*Je suis plein*' – you must say '*J'ai assez mangé*' (I've eaten enough). An English woman friend of mine once announced loudly at dinner '*Je suis pleine*,' and when everyone had stopped laughing, they explained that, basically, she was saying 'I *am a pregnant cow.*'

Sometimes it's really not the foreigners' fault, though. You have to be a pretty good linguist, for example, to know that it is OK to talk about the noun *un baiser*, a kiss, but that the same word as a verb means 'to screw'. You go out on a date, someone asks you how it went, you reply gallantly that you only kissed, and you end up bragging about getting laid. Suitors in Corsica get shot for less.

The French love playing around with these ambiguities. They adore the fact that the French word for the group of plants that includes melons, marrows and courgettes is *cucurbitacée*. The only reason they know the name of this group of plants is that it sounds as if they are saying '*cul-cul-bite-assez*' or 'arse-arse-dick-enough', a kind of linguistic orgy.

Another good double entendre is the French word *suspect* (the suspect in a crime), pronounced 'soos-pay', which could be misheard as *suce-pet* ('fart-sucker', presumably an old French rural trade). There is a saying '*Il vaut mieux être suspect que lèche-cul*' – I'd prefer to be a fart-sucker than an arse-licker. Yes, a typically meaningless French pun, but it shows how much they enjoy naughty pronunciation exercises. And discussing bodily functions.

Get Your Bouche Round This

A short guide to pronouncing those difficult French sounds:

- The open 'ou', as in *bouche* or *beaucoup*: imagine you are a chimpanzee with an unpeeled banana between your lips. Hold your mouth in that position and say 'oo'. Note: you don't have to scratch your armpits as you do this.

- The closed 'u', as in *rue*: imagine you are holding a cheap French cigarette between your lips. Push your top lip out until the cigarette is pointing vertically downwards and the tobacco is falling out of the end. Say 'oo'. It should sound almost like a short 'i' sound, as in 'hit'. It might help to get the pronunciation right if you squint as though the evil-smelling smoke is getting in your eyes.

- The 'an' and 'en' sounds, as in *quand*: imagine you have just been told the price of the *café au lait* you ordered on the Champs Elysées. Your jaw hangs open. You grunt in pain. Say the English word 'on' in this position, without pronouncing the 'n'.

- The 'on' sound, as in *bon*: you go to kiss a French man or woman on the lips, but you're afraid that tongues might get involved and you don't want that (yet). So you purse your lips but keep them firm. Again, say the English word 'on' in this position, without pronouncing the 'n'.

- The guttural 'r', as in *Sacrrrré Coeurrr*: imagine you are outside a French *boulangerie*, drooling at a superb fresh raspberry tart. Your mouth is suddenly full of saliva, and fortunately you are alone in the street so it is safe to spit in the gutter. Hawk it all up. As the saliva gathers underneath your tongue, you are saying the French 'r'. If you can hawk loudly enough, you are ready to become a French folk singer.

Some amusing but fairly meaningless mistakes you can make when speaking French

Try saying these pairs of phrases, if necessary using the pronunciation guide above. When you can spot the difference between the two versions, it is safe to go to France.

Mon chien vient de mourir.	My dog just died.
Mon chien vient de mûrir.	My dog just ripened.

Il est fou.	He is crazy.
Il est fût.	He is a beer barrel.

Comment s'appelle cette rue?	What's the name of this street?
Comment s'appelle cette roue?	What is the name of this wheel?

J'ai pu.	I was able to.
J'ai poux.	I have (ungrammatical) headlice.

Une bouée de sauvetage.	A lifebelt.
Une buée de sauvetage.	A lifesaving mist.

Je voudrais une table à l'ombre.	I'd like a table in the shade.
Je voudrais une table à l'ambre.	I'd like a table made of amber.

J'aimerais juste un baiser.	I just want a kiss.
J'aimerais juste baiser.	I just want to get laid.

CONTINUED...

Baisse-toi.	Duck your head down.
Baise-toi.	Screw yourself.
Tu pèses ('pez') combien?	How much do you weigh?
Tu baises ('bez') combien?	How much do you screw?
Il a trouvé la foi.	He has found faith.
Il a trouvé le foie.	He has found the liver.
Je vais faire un tour.	I'm going for a walk.
Je vais faire une tour.	I'm going to build a tower.
J'ai eu un malaise.	I felt ill.
J'ai eu une Malaise.	I shagged a Malaysian woman.

The nominees for last year's Most Imaginative
French Book Cover award.

THE
6TH
COMMANDMENT

Tu Ne Chanteras Pas
THOU SHALT NOT SING
(in tune, anyway)

THOU SHALT NOT SING
(in tune, anyway)

I HAVE TO START OUT BY STRESSING THAT I AM A HUGE FAN of (in no particular order) Matisse, Zola, Serge Gainsbourg, Ravel, Debussy, Les Rita Mitsouko, Flaubert, Juliette Binoche, Balzac, Django Reinhardt, Camus, Céline and old Jean Gabin movies. Comedy is my first love in culture, and I've enjoyed many a giggle at Voltaire, Boris Vian, the stand-up comedian Coluche, and joyful, unpretentious films like *La Cage aux Folles*, *Jour de Fête*, *Les Valseuses*, *La Belle Américaine*, *Papy Fait de la Résistance*, and *Le Grand Blond avec une Chaussure Noire*.

But all that is in the past, which is where French culture is stranded. It has been squatted by the middle-aged Paris Establishment that is scared to death of anything truly new and innovative because that would undermine the whole edifice.

These days, the most important ingredient in French culture is the navel. Artists, writers, singers and film directors spend their whole time gazing at it. Writers write books about being writers, directors make films about their latest failed love affair, singers listen to themselves moaning clever puns over non-existent tunes. They're all inside the Establishment and they have forgotten what life is like – or even that there is a life – outside. There is even a word for this in French – *nombrilisme*. 'Navelism' is so entrenched that it is an 'ism'.

And their excuse is: OK, it may be *merde*, but at least it's French *merde*. This too is in the dictionary. It's called *l'exception française*. Culture has to be good except if it's French. Zola, Matisse and co. must be turning in their graves. Voltaire would just giggle.

Popping the Bubble

The French think too much to be any good at making music. Music comes from the soul (or, where rock is concerned, from somewhere between the guts and the genitals), and the French rely too much on their brains.

I've played bass with lots of semi-professional bar bands, murdering everything from pub rock to salsa, and I've noticed one fundamental difference between French and 'Anglo-Saxon' musicians. If you want to start off a rehearsal with a jam to get to know each other, a Brit or American will say something like, 'OK, blues in E, one, two, three, four,' and you're away. The French will argue for ten minutes about who's going to come in first, what speed to play it, and what order to solo in.

This is why the French love to play and listen to jazz. It's thought music. I can busk along with pretty well any tune if you give me a minute to learn it, but I went for double-bass lessons with a French jazz bassist, and after every lesson I was playing worse. Instead of helping me busk along (which I thought was the point of jazz), he explained Greek scales and Ultrabionic harmonies or whatever, and I had to think so hard that I didn't dare touch the strings any more.

It's the same with kids' music lessons. At French schools, any child with a burning desire to learn the piano, the guitar or the drums will be forced to do a year's *solfège* (reading music) before they're allowed to get their hands on the instrument. This ensures that all the really passionate, impatient wannabe musicians (the ones likely to turn into a Hendrix or a Cobain) will give up and do volleyball instead.

Consequently, French pop music is, apart from a very few exceptions, excruciatingly painful. Short of finding a dead swan in my bathwater, there are few things that would make me jump out of a steaming tub in the middle of winter and dash across a freezing cold bathroom. But if I'm listening to the radio and a bad French pop song comes on, hypothermia seems a small price to pay for the relief of changing to a less offensive station.

And if you complain that a tune is rubbish or non-existent, you'll be told, *ah oui*, but the words are wonderful. Which is like saying that a bowl of soup tastes like dog's breath but looks sublime.

To give you an idea, here are a few recipes for French dog's breath soup – I mean, hit songs:

- Take a boring tune. Get a producer to dub grungy guitars over it to make it sound rocky. Write a list of twenty unrelated but similar-sounding words. Find a singer to mumble them throatily. Sell to French radio station.

- Take a cute ethnic-minority girl. Imitate the backing track to a recent American R&B hit. Get a rich Parisian to write some lyrics about how hard it is to survive in the poor suburbs. Sell to French radio station.

- Take an ageing star. Get him or her to sing any old nonsense. Call it a glorious comeback. Sell to French radio station.

- Take a below-averagely talented busker. Proclaim him as a poetic genius. Sell to French radio station.

The recipes can't fail because there is a legal quota system that obliges radio stations to play French music (as up to 40 per cent of their output, depending on what type of station it is), with an emphasis on 'new French production'. The message is clear – you slap any old *merde* on to a CD, and the radio will play it. You don't even need anyone to actually *like* your record, let alone buy it, because radio play generates plenty of income.

This is the driving force behind French pop music today.

It's not surprising that the musicians themselves have an image problem. They don't know what they're doing. One famous French singer thinks he's Radiohead, dresses like Jim Morrison, and writes songs like Andrew Lloyd Webber. Another dresses like a punk clown on stage and looks like a nerdy webmaster off it – hasn't he heard about living your music? At least old Serge Gainsbourg *always* looked like a human cigarette butt and sang almost exclusively about shagging. He understood image.

French music hasn't really known what it's up to since fake French Teddy Boys started singing translations of American rock 'n' roll songs at the end of the 1950s. These singers, with stage names like Johnny Hallyday, Eddy Mitchell and Dick Rivers, didn't understand the original words or the music. They were basically crooners with a quiff. Since then, you can count the number of decent French pop bands on one hand and still have enough fingers left over to hold your Gauloise.

This fundamental lack of understanding about pop music is good news for some people, though. The French have so little concept of the changing fashions in music that once an artist has cracked France, he or she will stay popular for ever. Eternal favourites here include Supertramp, the Cure, Jeff Buckley, Midnight Oil, Lenny Kravitz, Texas, Placebo and – most weirdly of all – eighties synth-popsters Cock Robin, who have probably earned enough from French radio plays of 'When Your Heart Is Weak' to retire to the Côte d'Azur.

Film for Film's Sake

In a typical French film, so an LA joke goes, Marc is in love with Sophie, Sophie loves François, François has the hots for Charlotte, who is in love with Isabelle, but Isabelle loves Gérard, who has a crush on Florence, who loves Marc. And in the end, they all go out to dinner.

Yes, modern French cinema can be a *soupçon* predictable.

Even so, the French are right to be proud of their film industry. Not necessarily of their films, but of the industry that makes them. They have a massive stock of experienced directors, writers, cameramen and technicians ready to leap into action, which they do with almost as much regularity as the movie production line in Bollywood.

And the reason is money. If they want to make a French movie, they can get cash to make it from the CNC (Centre National de la Cinématographie), a state-run institution that creams off a percentage of the box-office takings from the country's cinemas and dishes the money out to fund new films. A brilliant idea that enables small productions to get off the ground when they'd be doomed to failure in most other countries.

The trouble is that the system has also created a 'film for film's sake' mindset in France – let's make a film just to use up the grant money. The film doesn't have to earn much at the box office. With its grants and subsidies, and a probable TV showing or two, the very fact of making it is a pretty safe bet as long as the director doesn't blow millions on special effects. But then, who needs special effects when you can shoot a bunch of love scenes and marital arguments in a Paris apartment?

What's more, making the film is *doubly* profitable for everyone involved. French film-industry workers qualify as *intermittents du spectacle*, or occasional show-business workers. Once they have done their minimum number of hours' work for the year (507 in the previous twelve-month period), they qualify for unemployment money. And not just a token sum but their hourly salary, paid for all the time between jobs. So a film director who makes one feature film a year can get paid full-time at the hourly rate he charged while he was making the film. The same goes for everyone else involved, from the actors to the guys who screw together the camera tripods. Spend, say, three months making one bad film and you can live like a movie star for the rest of the year.

Not exactly a motivation to make good movies.

France has, of course, made some truly great movies. And most of them are great precisely because they are so French. Directors like Renoir, Godard, Truffaut, Chabrol and Blier could not have come from anywhere else on the planet. And France still manages to turn out the odd quirkily French art-house gem like *Delicatessen*, and the occasional unpretentious comedy like *Les Visiteurs*. So this system of keeping everyone in the movie industry on the national payroll has clearly paid off.

But these days, the industry seems to have lost its sense of experimentation and fun and decided to stick to filming its own navel. Here is a summary of a recent French film that shall remain nameless: 'Xavier decides to become a novelist, but in the meantime he has to take on a variety of jobs – journalist, scriptwriter, ghostwriter.' Yeah, right, very varied. In the sequel poor old Xavier will probably be forced (*horreur!*) to write short stories.

Directors who want to make something different go

abroad. Luc Besson (*The Fifth Element*) and Michel Gondry (*Eternal Sunshine of the Spotless Mind*) are Hollywood operators now. And when Besson makes something French but different, like the incredibly popular car-chase movie *Taxi*, he is looked down upon by the art establishment as a purveyor of crude, Hollywood-style non-art that he cynically aims at the American market.

This is, of course, total hypocrisy. If you gave truth serum to the snootiest French film director, the head of the 'I make French films and *merde* to everyone else' campaign, he or she would eventually break down and start sobbing, 'Why doesn't Hollywood want to adapt any of my films?'

Art for Fart's Sake

French artists can't get it out of their heads that this is the country of Renoir, Monet, Manet and Cézanne, and the place where foreigners like Picasso, Van Gogh, Modigliani, Giacometti and so many others came to develop their art. Instead of inspiring today's artists to follow their dream, though, this national heritage only encourages them to act like Picasso instead of painting like him.

Paris regularly holds studio open days, when whole *quartiers* of the city become artistic treasure hunts. You get a little map and follow directions to all the different artists' studios in the neighbourhood. And in almost every case, you'll find a place that looks like a real artist's studio (splodges of paint, ink, plaster or other materials you don't want to enquire about), and sounds like a real artist's studio (the drone of a voice explaining the art on show – although the best art doesn't need any explaining at all), but feels like a waste of time. The art on show will probably be either sub-Impressionist, supposedly 'shocking' or 'inspired' by a visit to some exotic corner of the world where the art is easily copyable.

I'm not saying that Damien Hirst sawing cows in half is the be-all and end-all of art, but at least it's different.

In any case, these days the most inventive French artists are much more interested in comic books, or BD ('bay-day', an abbreviation of *bande dessinée*), than straight art. But these should never be called 'comic books'. They are the *neuvième art*, and must be taken very seriously. And it is definitely not polite to say that the best BD artists are Belgian.

They've Got le Look

The French are convinced that they are the sexiest people on earth, apart perhaps from the odd Hollywood hunk or Brazilian beach babe. As proof, they will say that their *haute couture* is the most stylish in the world. Though this is rather like saying that the Koreans are the best drivers on earth because that's where so many cars are made. The truth is that the French mostly dress like frumps.

There are, of course, some incredibly sexy people walking the streets (and especially the beaches) of France. But this has more to do with their relative lack of obesity and an ability to resist the temptation to ruin their skin and hair with gallons of make-up and blond dye. When people write books about French women, they go on about style, taste and class. What they seem to mean is arch-conservatism. If you look at film divas like Sophie Marceau, Juliette Binoche or Carole Bouquet, you hardly notice their clothes. It's what is inside that counts. The clothes are usually as classic (a polite word for unadventurous) as you can get.

The average French person totally ignores the existence of French *haute couture*. Partly because *haute couture* is not really meant to be worn at all, of course – the catwalk designs are simply there to get photos into magazines. Partly also because even the *prêt à porter* stuff by Dior, Chanel, Yves Saint Laurent et al costs a fortune. But mainly because most French people prefer to dress like their mums and dads did, and fit into the traditional bourgeois mould.

French teenagers come in three basic models – the denim classic, the seventies hippy/fake Rasta and the sporty Bronx rapper/ho. When they cross over into adult life, though, they dispense with any daring elements and start dressing like their parents. As soon as male office workers hit their mid-twenties, they begin wearing ties that seem to have died of boredom. Meanwhile, their female colleagues will often dress as if looking for sympathy. Individual style is almost non-existent – it's as if no one wants to stand out from the crowd. Go to a party in Paris thrown by anyone over twenty-five and the likelihood is that most people in the room will be in jeans or dressed in black. The worst thing anyone in Paris can do is appear uncool, and wearing jeans or black is totally safe. If the clothes in question have a discreet French designer label, all the better, but the important thing is not to stand out in the crowd.

Yes, sorry, France. Apart from a few chic exceptions, you may dress to kill, but to kill with classicism.

And if the French are so stylish, how come the top French fashion houses employ British designers like Alexander McQueen and John Galliano, or Germans like Karl Lagerfeld?

Prozac of the People

In July 2004, the head of France's biggest commercial television channel, TF1, said that his programmes existed to sell Coca-Cola. Patrick Le Lay gave an interview declaring that TF1's programmes 'had a vocation to entertain the viewers and relax them between two commercial breaks'. And the astonishing thing is that despite this cynicism, his channel remained the most popular in the country, which says a lot about the discernment of the average French *téléspectateur*.

This flagrant desire to sell advertising space means that prime-time television in France is as exciting and varied as a nuns' shoe shop.

At eight o'clock in the evening, the two main channels, TF1 and France 2, have their evening news. At around eighty forty p.m., the news finishes and an endless series of ads, broken up by weather, lottery results and the like, begins. Meanwhile, the other main channels, which air their news at different times so as not to compete, will have caught up and will be ready to begin the big prime-time show. At ten to nine or so, this main attraction begins, and won't end until ten or ten thirty. If the viewers are lucky, it will be a movie, telefilm or documentary. More frequently, it will be either a reality TV show or some kind of panel game on which ageing stars and wit-less presenters will be given enormous microphones and told to laugh at each other's anecdotes or old TV clips.

In France, the big handheld microphone is much more than a phallic symbol – it is a badge that tells the viewer, 'I'm on TV and you're not, peasant.' The French do have lapel mics, but these are considered too small to be effective on the prime-time chat shows. Only if you are brandishing a silver cucumber will the viewer under-stand that you are a TV star and therefore by definition intelligent, witty and beautiful.

The French make good documentaries (which are, of course, on-screen opportunities to prove how right you are about something) and reasonable telefilms, espe-cially detective stories that give them a chance to per-petuate the myth that their police are good at solving crimes. On the other hand, French TV producers do not understand the sitcom. They do make them, but they are more sit than com. This is mainly because they think TV is not a noble medium, but just a pale imitation of a cinema screen, a bit like a postcard of the Mona Lisa.

Why 'waste' good writers and actors on something so short and frivolous?

But this attitude is just like France's relationship with the hamburger – it's not noble cuisine, but the French secretly binge on it whenever they can. At the time of writing there are three TV channels showing constant re-runs of *Friends*, sometimes two or three episodes back to back, to fill the yawning gap left by the lack of decent French programmes.

You Can Judge a Livre by Its Couverture

French literary books have the most boring covers since Moses carved the commandments on to bare stone. Even then, Moses probably chose a nice shade of grey rock for his tablets.

To be taken seriously, a *littéraire* novel must have a plain white cover with no decoration except for the title and the author's name in tiny lettering. Pale yellow is just about permissible, so long as it is a joyless hue, the dull shade of the wallpaper in a run-down old people's home. Anything more flamboyant would devalue the words inside, which are of such profound import that it is almost sacrilege to print them on such a lowly, opaque substance as paper. They should be etched on glass so that the reader can see them in all their blinding clarity.

That, at least, is the theory. In practice, a lot of this

grande littérature is pure *merde*. Either it's by a *grand auteur* who wrote one good book forty years ago and has been churning out the same old tripe ever since, or it's new, daring and experimental, i.e. totally unreadable. There will be large doses of '*oh mon dieu*, it's tough to be a writer' angst, microscopic examinations of human relationships that seem to be designed to put you off falling in love ever again, and attempts at innovative style that make the act of reading as pleasurable as pulling a truck through drying cement. With your eyelids. It's like France's worst films, but without the pictures.

This criticism may sound extreme, but if you've ever heard a snooty French literary novelist saying with mind-searing hypocrisy that (s)he doesn't care whether anyone actually buys his/her novel at all because the important thing is that (s)he has enriched the world with his/her art, then you would understand where I'm coming from.

On the other hand, French books with picture covers can be very good. They're great at historical novels and biographies, for example. Let no one accuse me of being totally negative.

Things to say if you want to provoke a French culture snob

Mon film préféré est *Terminator 2*.	*Mo film pray fairay ay* Termy Natt-or duh.	My all-time favourite film is *Terminator 2*.
Avez-vous déjà vu *Le Retour de la Panthère Rose*?	*Avay voo daydja voo l'Retoor da la Pon-tair Roz*?	Have you ever seen *Return of the Pink Panther*?
Truffaut, c'est une sorte de champignon, non?	*True-fo, set oon sort da shompee nyo, no*?	Truffaut? Isn't that a kind of mushroom?
Le CD est coincé, non?	*L' say-day ay kwan-say, no*?	Is the CD stuck?
Qu'est-ce que vous faites dans la vie, à part la peinture?	*Kes-ka voo fett dola vee ah par la pan-toor*?	What do you do apart from paint?
Je crois que ce livre a perdu sa couverture.	*Dje krwa ke se lee-vra ah pair-doo sa koov-air-toor.*	I think the cover has fallen off this book.
Avouez-le, en fait vous n'aimez pas ça, n'est-ce pas?	*A-voo-ay la, o fett voo nay-may pa sa, ness pa*?	Admit it – you don't really like this, do you?
C'est pour rire, non?	*Say poor rear, no*?	This is a joke, right?

'Sold', the sign says. What this British family don't know is that they've just agreed to pay two hundred thousand euros for a parasol.

THE
7TH
COMMANDMENT

Tu Ne Sauras Pas
THOU SHALT NOT KNOW

THOU SHALT NOT KNOW

I N FRANCE, THINGS ARE DONE ON A 'DON'T NEED TO KNOW' basis. Unless forced to do otherwise, no one will tell you anything.

There have been cases of people left sitting for hours on a motionless train in the middle of France, staring out at the fields of sweetcorn and wondering why they weren't using the rest of the railway line. Had the locomotive broken down? Was there a bomb or a cow on the line? Had the driver stopped off at a friend's house to watch the Tour de France? Nobody would say.

I once arrived at Charles de Gaulle airport to find that there were no immigration officials on duty. Two planeloads of jetlagged travellers crowded into the arrivals area, jostling for position in front of the unmanned booths, wishing they'd gone for a pee before getting off the plane, and waited for forty five minutes. There were no announcements, and no one to complain to. In the end a woman found out that there was a bomb scare at the airport by phoning a friend who worked in a café in the departure lounge. The officials finally turned up, everyone pushed forward with their passports, and no more was said about the wait.

The worst case I ever experienced was coming home to my apartment one afternoon to find a masked, body-armoured, machine-gun-toting policeman on my landing. At least I hoped he was a policeman.

'What's going on?' I asked, rather bravely, I thought.

'You don't need to know,' he said.

I didn't feel like arguing.

Sometimes, the French complain about this ambient secrecy, but there are lots of things they actually prefer to keep quiet. They hate being spied upon – mainly because they have so many guilty secrets.

There are very few CCTV cameras in France, and the French are very smug about this. They know that they would only get caught driving badly, walking furtively into a hotel with their lover, letting their dog poo on the pavement, dumping their leaky car battery on a street corner, or doing a whole variety of other antisocial things. So what if a few muggings and car thefts go unsolved?

The funniest example of strategic secrecy is a French itemized phone bill, which never gives the complete numbers called. It gives the first six digits, but not the rest, so that jealous spouses cannot call numbers they don't recognize and get through to a lover.

This is why secrecy is tolerated. You keep your secret, I'll keep mine. A*u revoir*.

Danger? What Danger?

On the north-west tip of Normandy, just fifteen miles from the Channel Islands, is a typical French secret. It's a place whose existence is not denied at all – the area's official website provides a link to '*un autre site*' about the region, which has a very informative page on the subject.

But when you click on the link, you think, holy *merde*, why does no one talk about this?

This place is Cap de la Hague, a nuclear reprocessing plant much like the one at Sellafield in the north-west of England, which is so notorious that its name keeps getting changed to try and throw the public off the scent (people with long memories may recall that in the past it's also been called Seascale and Windscale). But Cap de la Hague has always been Cap de la Hague. And unlike Sellafield, which regularly has the whole of Britain and Ireland up in arms about pollution, Cap de la Hague is ignored. Even though there is also a massive conventional nuclear power station right next to it.

This silence is all the more surprising (or, cynics would say, less surprising) because the site is right in the middle of a summer tourist area. Practically every coastal town within a hundred miles is a seaside resort where people happily swim, paddle and fish for shrimps. The bay to the west is a big oyster-producing region, and Le Mont Saint Michel is just seventy miles downwind.

The reason is that France is the only country in the world, apart from North Korea, where nuclear power is totally safe. The whole country is miraculously protected from any likelihood of radiation poisoning or fallout. When the cloud of luminous dust floated across Europe from Chernobyl in 1986, it famously stopped at the French border. Farms just across the line in Germany, Switzerland and Italy were polluted and sales of their produce embargoed, but in France crops were untouched.

It is the same for asbestos. It is only in the past decade or so that asbestos has officially become dangerous in France. Before that, it was perfectly safe, and the students of the asbestos-ridden university building at Jussieu in central Paris were in no danger whatsoever from the particles they kicked about and inhaled as they walked the corridors.

Could all this be because certain French companies are (or were, in the case of asbestos) amongst the world's biggest manufacturers of these allegedly toxic materials? *Mais non!*

Astonishingly, the French don't seem to mind this at all. For one thing, they have more important matters to think about than whether some factory they can't see, hear or smell might be polluting the beach where they have decided to spend their holiday. For another, they are a technological people and believe that the Earth would be a better place if engineers ran the world and left everyone else to get on with the more refined things in life.

Je Ne Sais Quoi

Conspiracies of silence work very well in France because the country is indeed run by technocrats, most of whom went to school with each other. Many of the politicians, industrialists and financiers, and even some of the supposedly independent press barons, come from the elite *grandes écoles*. The country echoes to the sound of these people scratching each other's backs. Three French presidents in a row – Giscard d'Estaing, Mitterrand and Chirac – have been either openly accused of crimes or tainted by dubious friendships, but continued their careers. And Charles de Gaulle is quoted as saying that 'a politician so rarely believes what he is saying that he is astonished when anyone believes him'. It's not surprising that the French are completely cynical about their leaders.

This impenetrability helps them to be subtly efficient on the world stage.

They somehow manage to extricate French hostages from Iraq with their heads still attached to their shoulders. They deny that this is because they pay the hostage-takers, and no one believes them, but they don't care.

They howl about globalization, which they refuse to call globalization, even though it would be a perfectly acceptable French word – instead they have coined the alternative *mondialisation*. They spit with fury if a foreign company tries to buy out a big French firm – in the case of Danone, the government actually blocked the deal – yet they lambast the USA about its protectionism. And meanwhile, the French export their nuclear power stations, car plants, trains and food technology, much of which is directly or indirectly subsidized by the government. Millions of Brits drink water supplied by French companies. And all over the world, even as far away as Sydney, you will see bus stops built by Decaux, the genius who conceived the idea of paying to build bus stops and then taking the revenue from on-site advertising. It's a slow, silent invasion, kept semi-secret by the way the French continually complain that their economy is collapsing and the whole world is against them. A brilliant cover-up.

Don't Mention the War

The Nazi occupation of France really traumatized the nation. Not so much because they suddenly had men in jackboots marching about the place, but because so many French people went over to the other side.

At the end of the war, lots of collaborators were executed, and women who'd consorted with the enemy had their heads shaved. But these were only the people who didn't have enough influential friends to cover them. Some of the worst collaborators were never tried or even accused. Meanwhile, amongst the genuine heroes on the official lists of *Résistants*, there were people who had never lifted a finger against the Nazis.

The best example of these postwar double standards was a woman called Marthe Richard. She is famous in

France as the crusader who closed down all the brothels in the country in 1946, ostensibly because they were health hazards and hotbeds of organized crime, and had often welcomed the Occupying Forces with open arms (and open other limbs, too). She was chosen to spearhead the clean-up campaign because she was a heroine of the *Résistance*, a national figurehead. However, it was later alleged that the supposedly saintly Madame Richard had herself been a Madame during the war, and had worked with pro-Nazi gangsters as well as organizing sex parties for the Gestapo. Moral confusion at its most French.

This trauma explains why there are no TV programmes like *Crimewatch* in France. The French say this would be a call for the public to denounce possible innocents. Which is what so many of them were doing from 1940 to 1944.

But it's all hypocrisy. They do denounce people to the authorities, every day.

I lived for a while in a building where a man was caught stealing electricity. He had bypassed his meter, but had left the earth wire hanging loose near a water pipe. The trick was discovered when his next-door neighbour turned on the tap one day and flew across the kitchen with her hair on fire. The electricity men came, the fraudster was prosecuted, and the following year the neighbour was visited by tax inspectors who went through all her books and bank accounts. Someone had told the taxman that she was earning undeclared income working from home. It was not difficult to guess who.

Denouncing people can even be a negotiating tactic. A shower in a tiny studio apartment on the floor above me leaked into my living room because the landlord had installed it on bare floorboards. The tenant had no insurance because the landlord was not declaring the rent and so refused to issue a lease, which is necessary for a tenant to get home insurance. My insurance man told me to blackmail the landlord into paying for the damage and fixing the shower immediately by threatening to shop him to the taxman. *Charmant*, I thought. The threat worked like a dream, though.

Lawyers against the Law

French court lawyers all look like abstract sculptors who have been practising on their own hair. They are often interviewed on TV about a case as their client enters or emerges from the courtroom, and they all look like the last person you would want to defend you in a court of law. Unshaven, vaguely psychopathic, totally untrustworthy.

But in fact they are often very astute operators, because they are experts at manipulating French secrecy.

In the British legal system, solicitors are officers of the court and as such are duty-bound to produce any relevant documents in their possession, even if they are harmful to their client. But French lawyers have no such obligation. So what if their client filmed himself hacking his business partner to death? No one else knows about the home slasher movie, so they can plead not guilty. At the same time, these lawyers are more than happy to review all the evidence into a forest of TV and radio mics and then claim that their client cannot possibly get a fair trial because the media keep reporting the case. The moral is, what better person to defend you than someone capable of such beautiful hypocrisy?

The Law in Inaction

The French police are divided into a variety of semi-independent bodies – the *police nationale*, who are run by the Ministry of the Interior, the *gendarmerie nationale*, who are part of the Ministry of Defence, the CRS (the gladiator-style riot police), the *police judiciaire*, the GIR (rapid intervention force), and others. But in French minds, they are more meaningfully divided into the ones who look silly and the ones who don't.

The ones who look silly include certain *gendarmes* who have to wear the old kepi, and the gangs of hickish beat cops who wander the streets of Paris looking as if they've failed the audition to become New York policemen because of their sloppy uniform. Even the CRS look quite silly before they put on their body armour, because of their shiny blue catsuits that zip up from the crotch.

These silly-looking units have a bad public image. The common perception is that the CRS do nothing but bludgeon students and union activists, and that the *gendarmes* and uniformed beat cops bumble about, allowing major crimes to disappear unsolved into a quagmire of paperwork.

But in fact, the less-than-serious cops are there to deflect attention from the more discreet ones. There are often brief stories in the newspapers about huge networks of fraud, internet crime or prostitution being cleared up. No fuss, lots of arrests, the suspects deported or sent to rot in jail. Individual crime may not concern the French police very much (if you get burgled, that's your headache), but give them a whole network to dismantle and their intelligence services spring silently into action. If the network involves influential people, it may not be dismantled quite so quickly, but that's a different problem.

The uniformed cops get their dramatic crime-busting operations, too, but they tend to net slightly smaller fish. Every weekend, there are crowds of French police on the Italian border, confiscating fake Dior T-shirts, cheap plastic imitations of Louis Vuitton bags and other counterfeit luxury items. These aren't being smuggled in by dealers, just by locals who nip over to Italy to get a chic brand-name jacket for a hundredth of the genuine price. The *gendarmes* stop cars that have been seen parked at Ventimiglia market by spies who are on the payroll of the big brands involved. The spies phone in the car registration numbers to the *gendarmes*, and the shoppers are stopped and dispossessed as soon as they cross back into France. On top of this, whole coachloads of naïve daytrippers are searched and relieved of their contraband.

They are absurdly easy pickings. And while this is going on, you could smuggle through a carload of white slaves, rocket-propelled grenade launchers or heroin – as long you are not a big enough fish to interest the secret services, of course. And as long as you're not wearing a fake Cartier watch.

Argent? What Argent?

One subject that the French feel uncomfortable talking about in polite society is money. Or rather, *their* money.

If you've got it, you shut up about it. Only the poor and the vulgar discuss how much they paid for something or how much they earn. And only the *nouveaux riches* wear huge watches and drive silly red sports cars.

This, though, is less out of polite discretion than fear.

France has a wealth tax that applies to everything you own, from your house and car to your post-office savings account. And it kicks in at a very low threshold. If you own a family-sized apartment in the centre of Paris, you really ought to be paying the *impôt sur la fortune* (ISF). I was once at a dinner party at the home of a Paris family who'd just had a lift installed in their building near the Seine. They were on the fifth floor, so the value of their apartment had gone up by at least 20 per cent, almost certainly taking it over the ISF threshold. An English woman at the party asked how much the place was worth now. The hostess blanched and went into etiquette shock. She felt that she ought to be polite and answer her guest, but at the same time it was an unspeakably blunt question for a dinner party, rather like asking how many lovers the hostess currently had on the go. I intervened, told the hostess that it was a very British question, and led the conversation away to safer dinner-party territory – how many lovers *other* people had on the go. Given that lots of comfortably-off city-dwellers own an apartment plus a country house and a couple of decent cars, they have to keep their heads down. Walking around in a Louis Vuitton leather overcoat and buying Dior sunglasses for the poodle would be worse than vulgar – it would be financial suicide.

This explains why the French are so good at inverted snobbery. Just as French artists will claim (untruthfully) that they don't care if no one buys their paintings, the rich are very skilled at looking poor. Or trying to, anyway.

I have spent a couple of summers on the île de Ré, just off the west coast of France, which is the country's capital of inverted snobbery. Everyone who's anyone in Paris has a house there, but none of them want to talk about it – the island is so trendy that house prices have become absurd. And you pay ISF on the *potential* value of your belongings, not the cash you get if you sell. Consequently, the rich Parisians try to blend in with the locals (and simultaneously disassociate themselves from the holidaymakers who rent places for the summer or – horrors – stay at campsites on the island). Look closely at that weatherbeaten fisherman walking along the *quai* at the swanky port of Saint Martin en Ré and you'll see that his faded shirt has a Ralph Lauren label, his shapeless shorts are by Lacoste and those deck shoes are in fact battered Gucci loafers. He might have arrived at the *quai* in an ancient Citroën 2CV or – even more chic – on a rusting pushbike, but this is only because his discreetly powerful Renault is in the tumbledown garage beside his island house. And if Johnny Depp were to ask him where the nearest chocolate shop was, he would snootily tell him to enquire at the nearest *office de tourisme*.

It's not that the rich Frenchman *wants* to be invertedly snobbish, you understand. He has to do it to protect his wealth. *Richesse oblige.*

Skeletons in the Cupboard

Housebuying is another subject shrouded in secrecy.

France makes the process less nerve-racking than it is in some other countries, with its system of signing a *promesse de vente* or *compromis de vente* – an agreement to buy, with a seven-day cooling-off period for the buyer. Once this is signed, the seller cannot accept any better offers. It is a great protection against gazumping, but even so, buyers can fall victim to a web of secrecy.

Of course, when buying a home, the French hire solicitors to make sure that there are no plans to run a motorway through the kitchen. They also demand to see proof that the building is not infested with termites or riddled with *amiante* (asbestos). But almost no one commissions a structural survey to make sure that the place is not simply going to fall down of its own accord. I mentioned the possibility of surveying the building when I bought my first small apartment in Paris, and the estate agent looked at me as if I'd just asked for proof that the world wasn't flat. In any case, if I'd found someone to do a survey, and discovered that all the supporting walls in the building had been removed and the place was being held up by the telephone cables, it would have done me no good. The agent would simply have replied, OK, so do you want to buy it or not? If not, no problem, because the next set of potential buyers won't commission a survey.

Instead, I have found it useful to go around an apartment with a builder while the agent or seller is present. The builder can then poke at things, measure damp and stare inscrutably into corners, uttering the odd meaningful 'hmmmm' and questions like 'And when exactly was this doorway put in?' This direct, less administrative, more secretive method can scare the sellers, and helped me negotiate a big discount on my second, larger, apartment. I went into a huddle with the builder and put in a low offer, without explaining why, and it was accepted. Two can play at the secrecy game.

In small towns, if the seller of a house or land has friends in the town hall, all manner of undesirable facts can be covered up or forgotten. How else would so many houses be sold in flood zones in the Languedoc? And why did Monsieur Dupont get permission to add an extra storey on to his cottage, and the estate agent assure the prospective buyers of the house next door that they would be able to do the same, when permission was refused out of hand once the deal was done? Or, even worse, why did the *mairie* send you a letter saying that your entire barn conversion was not *conforme*, and demanding that said barn be demolished, the day after you bought it?

The answer is an open secret – the best protection against getting caught out is to do your own research.

It sounds incredibly obvious, but you have to go and see the property. Even if you know you're buying a ruin with no electricity, how can you be sure that your pile of stones doesn't look out over an out-of-town industrial estate? The French are great fans of blighting their countryside with a splattering of furniture warehouses, hypermarkets and roadside restaurants. Then again, there are probably people who dream of a conservatory with an uninterrupted – and very French – view of Conforama, Carrefour and Buffalo Grill.

If you're buying in a village, it's a good idea to go to the *mairie* and make enquiries about past planning applications for your prospective property, and present ones for the neighbouring houses or fields.

If you're buying an apartment, it is essential to delve into the minutes of past owners' meetings. These *compte-rendus des réunions de copropriété* will reveal everything the seller and estate agent want to keep quiet.

Perhaps the owners voted against renovating the facade of the building (known as a *ravalement*), even though the building's agents (the *syndic*) warned them that the city would force them to carry it out the following year, when it would be even more expensive. A *ravalement* can cost each owner thousands of euros, and this alone will convince some people to sell their apartment, with all its hidden future liabilities.

Perhaps someone proposed installing a lift, but the city refused to authorize it because the building is over 150 years old and cannot be structurally altered. When you read this in the *compte-rendu*, the seller's assurance that the staircase is wide enough for a lift and that the other owners are all in favour counts for nothing.

Maybe the *syndic* is so fed up with the owners opposing any outlay on upkeep that it is going to terminate its contract and leave the building without agents to manage its affairs.

All this will be there in the minutes. Their revelations about a building's secret life can be absolutely riveting. And can save housebuyers from making total fools of themselves.

Some French phrases to use when trying to find out the truth about the house or apartment you are planning to buy

Où est la centrale nucléaire/station d'épuration/porcherie la plus proche?	*Oo-ay la sontraal noo-klay-air/stass-eeo day-poo-rassyo/ porshery la ploo prosh?*	Where is the nearest nuclear power station/sewage works/pig farm?
Pourquoi la maison/ l'appartement est en vente?	*Pork-wa la mayzo/ lapartmo ett oh vont?*	Why is the house/ apartment being sold?
Le même notaire ne représente pas le vendeur et l'acheteur, j'espère?	*Le mem no-tair ne r'pray-zont pa l'vonderay lash-ter djess-pair?*	The same solicitor is not acting for both buyer and seller, I hope?
Avez-vous une carte des zones inondables?	*Avay voo oon carrt day zonn eenon-dah-bla?*	Do you have a map of the flood zones?
Je voudrais visiter avec mon maçon.	*Dje voodray veezeetay avek mo masso.*	I'd like to visit the place with my builder.

CONTINUED...

C'est quoi, cette fissure dans le mur/ cette tache au plafond/ce trou dans le plancher?	*Say kwa set fishoor doh l'moor/set tasho plaffo/stroo doh l'plonshay?*	What is that crack in the wall/stain on the ceiling/hole in the floor?

(All the ingredients are of course interchangeable – you can have a fissure in the plafond and the plancher, too.)

C'est quoi, cette odeur dans l'escalier?	*Say kwa set o-deurr doh less-kallee-ay?*	What is that smell on the staircase?

Qui habite au-dessus/en-dessous/ à côté/en face?	*Kee a-beet oh-dassoo/on dassoo/ ah kotay/on fass?*	Who lives upstairs/ downstairs/next door/opposite?

(Given the difficulty in differentiating between dessus and dessous, it is best to point at the same time.)

Est-ce qu'il y a des projets de réparation du toit/de la façade/ de l'escalier?	*Esskeel ya day prodjay d'rayparassyo doo twa/d'la fassad/ d'less-kally-ay?*	Are there any plans to repair the roof/ facade/staircase?

Est-ce que les travaux ont été votés?	*Esske lay travo ontettay votay?*	Has the work been approved by a vote of the building's co-owners?

(If so, the seller pays, not the buyer.)

CONTINUED...➤

Pouvez-vous me montrer une preuve/un certificat/un bail/un contrat/ l'acte de propriété/ une pièce d'identité/l'argent?	*Poovay voo m'montray oon preuv/uh sairtee-fika/uh ba-ee/uh kontra/lack d'propree-aytay/ oon pee-ess dee dontitay/lar-djo?*	Can you show me proof/a certificate/a lease/a contract/the deeds/some ID/the money?
Est-ce qu'il y a eu un permis de construire pour la piscine/la terrasse/ l'étage supplémentaire/ la maison?	*Esskeel ya-oo uh pair-mee d'konstweer por la piss-een/la tayrass/lay-taadj sooplay-montair/ lamayzo?*	Was planning permission obtained for the swimming pool/ terrace/extra storey/house?

The Paris tourist office provides a unique service for tourists who want to take a souvenir home on their shoes.

THE
8TH
COMMANDMENT

Tu N'aimeras Pas Ton Voisin
THOU SHALT NOT LOVE
THY NEIGHBOUR

THOU SHALT NOT LOVE
THY NEIGHBOUR

THE FRENCH ARE PROUD OF BEING INDIVIDUALISTIC. THEY present this as proof that they have *caractère*, rather than being bland pack animals like English football fans and all Scandinavians. In fact, though, what they're really trying to do is provide a philosophical justification for not giving up their seat to a pregnant woman on the bus.

This isn't entirely fair. France has a greater sense of solidarity than lots of countries around it. The French pay high taxes and social-security contributions, which go to provide high pensions, high unemployment benefits and excellent medical cover. They have a law – *non-assistance à personne en danger* – that makes it illegal not to help someone who is being mugged or crying for help through the door of their apartment, at least by phoning for assistance. It is illegal to evict a rent-defaulting tenant in winter, or to cut off their electricity. It is almost impossible to write your children out of your will. And, as we saw in the Second Commandment, even in the midst of a long transport strike, workers stick together.

But inside this comfort blanket, the French enjoy the feeling of being on a solo crusade against the system and everyone else in the world.

Lycée-faire

The classic theory is that this individualism comes from their peasant background – practically all French families need go back only two or three generations to find farmers who had to battle not only against cheese buyers and plough salesmen but also against the elements themselves. But that's a bit like saying that every French person should know how to milk a goat. In fact, they (modern French people, not goats) are rigorously trained in individualism at school. For a start, schools have no uniforms at all, so it's every brand name for itself. Children can dress how they want (except if they want to wear religious symbols). At the age of eleven, they are thrown into the *collège*, a junior high school for eleven- to fourteen-year-olds. Few will have the same timetable as their friends as this depends on what subjects they take, and they will often begin and end school at different times every day. Things get even worse for fifteen-year-olds at the *lycée*, when the school day has virtually no structure. In some schools they can even smoke in the playground. It is total *laissez-faire*. What's more, every time there are *baccalauréat* sessions or mock exams, many schools are emptied and pupils of all ages are thrown out on to the street and left to their own devices.

At university, life gets even more survivalist. In a spirit of so-called democracy, universities accept anyone with the *baccalauréat* who wants to sign up (and whose mum is prepared to stand in line for hours on registration day). So classrooms, or amphitheatres, are overfull, and students have to fight for a seat or stand at the back. The tutor, meanwhile, if he or she is not on strike or absent doing better-paid research, will turn up, talk into a microphone and then disappear.[30] And that's pretty well all the guidance new students get for at least the first year, when half of them will be kicked out for failing their exams because they didn't get enough guidance. Darwin himself could not have invented a more efficient way of turning young French people into lone rangers.

This system does have one major advantage, though. Because school life is so unstructured, young people spend much more time concentrating on their extra-curricular life. In the gaps in their school timetable, they will have had hours to talk about and practise seduction. They will have learned how to smoke convincingly and hang out in cafés just like the grown-ups. And because they generally stay at home with mummy and daddy till they're at least twenty-five, they can practise living the adult lifestyle without the actual stress of

. . . .

[30] There are also so-called TD (*travaux dirigés*) and TP (*travaux pratiques*) – smaller, supervised classes. But if a student doesn't turn up, no tutor is going to bother hassling a slacker and create extra work for him or herself.

finding a job and somewhere to live. They can lie back on their comfort blanket and concentrate on *moi*.

Je Fume, Moi Non Plus

I once read a novel set in France where the author had a character walk past a Parisian café and smell the coffee. But generally, if you can smell anything it is smoke. In some places, the no-smoking area is only a table away from the smokers, or consists of a few tables near the bar, where everyone stands and smokes.

If you are eating next to a table of smokers, you might as well order the *tabac* salad, the *ash du jour* and a *Gauloise brûlée* for dessert, because some people smoke one cigarette with their aperitif and light up again as soon as they finish each course. And if you try to tell them that you would quite like to taste your meal rather than their cigarette, you will often get a gruff reply about how they have the right to live the way they want to live and the rest is your problem. I know Americans in Paris who have major difficulties putting up with this kind of atmosphere. Smoking has been banned in so many places for so long back home that passive smoking is as outrageous to them as someone spitting on your plate.

One Californian occasionally tries the UN-sanction approach. 'You're not going to smoke any more!' he tells baffled French smokers, who wonder what he is going to do about it. Invade their table, maybe? This frontal attack never works. At best it causes a colonial war.

A New Yorker tries a more surreal approach. With his wonderfully American accent and a friendly smile, he tells cigar smokers, 'Thank you so much for smoking that near me. Now I can tell everyone back home that Europeans smoke donkey *merde*.' This method is satisfying, but equally pointless, because a Frenchman in a café does not give a donkey *merde* what Americans think of him.

The best method is to smile politely, say *'bonjour'* and tell the smoker that although they of course have the right to smoke and live the way they please, you would greatly appreciate it if they could try to direct their smoke away from you because you would like to enjoy your meal, and your life, undisturbed by their cigarette. A friendly-sounding appeal to respect your lifestyle is the only way to get things done.

France is heading for an existential crisis over smoking. Women and young people are cutting back, but the hardcore of heavy smokers are hanging steadfastly on to their habit, which is cheap, cool and still not frowned upon by the general public.

This might soon change, though. Smoking is already forbidden in aeroplanes, buses, many trains and metro stations, and there are plans afoot to ban it in all public places. If this should happen, the new law will almost certainly be ignored. Petty French laws are usually considered to be for other people, not for *moi*. What's more, any ban will cause the *buralistes*, the people who sell cigarettes, to go on strike and demand compensation for their lost income. There will almost certainly be protest marches in the streets (very slow marches, of course, so the demonstrators don't get out of breath). So there's a good chance the government will back down, or make the law so fuzzy that no one has to obey it if they don't want to.

But this habit of smoking in restaurants begs a very simple question: the French claim to love fine food, but how on earth do they taste it? Perhaps that's why they say that British and American food is so bland – there's no nicotine in it.

Not Waiting for Godot

The French think that queues are for people who have time to waste, whose lives are so boring that they have nothing better to do. Waiting in line is an admission of defeat.

At bus stops, taxi ranks, cafés or almost anywhere where queueing is not imposed by barriers, the French will not wait patiently. Queueing barriers have only been introduced in the past few years, and the depressed look on the faces of Parisians who are obliged by little plastic posts and lengths of polyester to wait their turn proves how tough it is for them to give up their habit of pushing in.

I remember the first time I saw this system in operation in Paris. It was in the food hall of the old Marks & Spencer shop at Châtelet. There were three or four tills, and customers simply chose the shortest queue. Then one evening, when I went to buy my digestive biscuits and raspberry trifle, there was a kind of corral where we all had to wait for the first till to be free. The Brits adopted the system instantly, especially because there was a notice on a little stand saying 'Queue here', and we expats are usually pretty disciplined, old-school folk. The French, though, were totally lost. You could see it in their eyes as they read the sign. They were thinking, 'Why should I wait back there behind that man holding the biscuits and that ridiculous English dessert when there is a till in front of me that is going to be free in ten seconds?' Some of them simply ignored the system and pushed in (accompanied by much British huffing and cries of 'That's not cricket,' of course). Others surrendered, shamefacedly went to the back of the line and tried not to look French.

Shortly afterwards, M&S pulled out of France. The newspapers said it was for group strategy reasons, but I'm sure it had something to do with trying to introduce obligatory queueing in Paris too soon.

The barriers have now been put up in most large post offices, which is a good thing, because the most spectacular piece of queue-jumping I have ever seen happened in a Paris post office without barriers.

It was at the 24/7 office in the rue du Louvre. I was there on a Sunday morning with a trolleyload of books to send off. Stupidly, I'd had a lie-in, and when I got across town at eleven a.m., there was a long, winding line of about twenty people waiting to go up to one of only two open windows. They were standing slightly back from the counter, as if to make it clear that the person at the front had the option of moving left or right according to which window became free first. Things were moving very slowly, and everyone was itching with impatience. The air was thick with expectation, eyes flicking around as people looked for an opportunity to push in or stop someone else doing so.

Then a woman walked in, a chic type with a leather jacket, high heels and a black ponytail. She took one look at the line of losers and marched straight up to stand behind the person getting served at one of the windows. A howl of protest went up.

'What are you all doing standing there?' she asked scornfully. 'I come here all the time and no one ever queues like that. We just go to stand in front of one of the windows.' She turned her back on the protesters, and three seconds later the long queue had self-destructed and there were two lines, one at each window. The social experiment had failed.

The post-office workers didn't intervene, of course. It wasn't their problem. And anyway, French officials are too concerned with looking cool to enforce petty regulations.

This is also true at airports. At a French airport, if the airline announces that a flight will begin boarding by rows 40–57, absolutely everyone goes forward to board. And the ground staff will often let everyone through. So if you are trying to reach your seat in row 57, when you finally get on the plane you'll be held up by a couple blocking the aisle in row 12 as they try to ram their oversized hand luggage into the overhead compartment, a man laying out his newspapers, computer and palm pilot in row 16 ready for his work session after take-off, and similarly infuriating queue-jumpers in rows 21, 25, 30, and 34.

If you try this trick at an American airport, though, you'll be turned back and told to wait until your row is called. I once watched a semi-organized line degenerate into a rugby scrum as French passengers came up against American ground staff when boarding an Air France Miami–Paris flight. People with boarding cards for the unannounced rows shoved forward, were turned back and then loitered at the front of the line so that they would be first on board when their time came, or even earlier if they saw the people checking row numbers give in to the pressure and let just one passenger on prematurely. The queue spread out and broke up rather like a tide of Tour de France cyclists ramming into the back of a crashed truck. Soon the whole section of departure lounge had been turned into an impenetrable jam. Thanks to the French passengers, a technique to make boarding smoother had produced total anarchy.

Again, it's all about *moi*, my life, my lifestyle. If yours were important, you would be trying to push in front of me instead of standing like a cow waiting for its turn at the abattoir. France's real motto is Liberté, Egalité, Get out of My Way.

Drive Me Crazy

Red lights are, of course, just another form of queue. So the French attitude to them is simple – they are only there to keep me from doing my really important stuff. And French drivers have two other philosophical reasons to ignore red lights. First, like condoms, they were invented by some fusspot who thinks I don't know how to look after myself. Second, if I decide it's safe to run the light, it's safe – I'm French, so I know best.

All this makes driving in France a hair-raising business.

I once had to drive from Siena to Florence airport (yes, geography fans, I've switched to Italy now). I was nervous about this, partly because I was alone and this was before there were little satellite devices in cars to tell you when to turn left and right, but mostly because I'd been fed the myth that Italians are the worst drivers in Europe.

The myth, I soon realized, was just that. I got hopelessly lost in Florence, swerved and weaved my way across lanes and junctions, drove the wrong way down a one-way street, stalled while trying to read my map in the middle of a roundabout, and yet I survived unscathed. The Italians seemed to be prepared for other drivers to behave like lunatics, and happy to let them get on with it.

In France (or Paris, anyway) I would have ended up in hospital and/or the wreckers' yard.

Parisian drivers not only drive like lunatics, they are also completely intolerant of other lunatics. I recently took a taxi from Charles de Gaulle airport into Paris, and the driver was a living example of this double lunacy. The traffic was heavy, and as we passed a turn-off for Le Bourget exhibition centre, cars were zig-zagging across the lanes like drunken puppies.

'Look, one of these people is going to cause an accident,' my driver said, accelerating straight into the path of a car that was clearly determined to cut him up. 'Did you see that?' he asked when I awoke from my dead faint. 'He nearly caused an accident.'

In some countries, it's the brake that keeps drivers out of trouble. In France, it's the accelerator. The driver who manages to look mad and dangerous enough will win through every time. He will probably get killed smashing into the back of a truck while doing 200kph through black ice on a foggy day (his last words 'What was that idiot trucker doing out on the roads on a day like this?'), but before then he will be *le roi de la route*.

Ironically, these huge pile-ups are even worse in summer, when French individualism behind the wheel is combined with the holiday herd instinct. Almost every car owner in the country heads for the motorway on one of six Saturdays in summer – the first weekends in July and August, the weekends closest to the bank holidays in mid-July and mid-August, and the last weekends of both months. These six *grands départs* are for the suicidal only. The jams on the main roads are like hundred-mile-long queues, with all the trauma that this implies for the French psyche. The picnic basket is probably full of wine, ideal for relaxing the frustrated driver. The kids are fighting in the back seat. And the *imbécile* in front is trying to cause an accident. It's just too tempting for French drivers. They feel almost honour-bound to get into a smash.

After all, what do you expect from a nation whose favourite spectator sport is the Tour de France, a three-week traffic jam?

Walk on the Wild Side

As a Parisian pedestrian, I often get the feeling that I am flying in a pheasant costume in front of a line of men with shotguns. And the bad news is that, like pheasants on a shooting estate, I can be mown down quite legally. Because Parisian pedestrian crossings are not like those in other countries. In Paris, you're not actually supposed to cross, even when the little man is green.

Here's how it works: imagine a crossroads with traffic lights. The lights go red on the east and west sides, and the little men go green for the pedestrians there. At exactly the same time, the lights go green for cars on the north and south sides. Consequently, the pedestrians are fair game for drivers turning right or left. There is nothing to force these drivers to stop for the pedestrians, except the flailing arms of those attempting to cross, pointing vainly at the tiny green man as cars screech round the corner towards them. When you add to this all the cars that run the red light, or who were (illegally) stuck halfway across the junction and drive through after the lights change, you realize why some junctions are only safe to cross on foot if you're a pole vaulter.

And that's with the supposed protection of the little green man. The black and white stripes painted on to road surfaces where there are no lights are regarded by most drivers as nothing more than horizontal graffiti. No Parisian driver ever stops at these. I was once sitting at a café terrace opposite one of these fake pedestrian crossings. A pregnant lady was waiting hopefully on the pavement, wondering whether she'd be able to get across the road before her baby arrived, when suddenly a car stopped spontaneously. A wave of surprise rippled across the terrace, and a woman at the table next to me murmured, *'un provincial'*. And sure enough, when the driver pulled away, the car had a 44 registration number – Brittany.

Outside Paris, drivers do stop for pedestrians without being forced to by traffic lights, a roadblock or a gun pointed at their windscreen. In summer, when the Parisians are on holiday, you can see them crossing the road, staring at the courteous local drivers with a mixture of surprise, gratitude and scorn: 'Why is this provincial stopping for me? Doesn't he have anywhere to go?'

This is the key to dangerous driving in France. Again, it's all about lifestyle. I, French driver, am in my car to go somewhere incredibly important. I have to hurry to my workplace so that I can get to the coffee machine at the same time as my cute new colleague, arrive at my holiday home in time for dinner, or get to the super-market before it closes. You, other driver, pedestrian, traffic light, are in the way of my lifestyle. Watch out, here I come.

A Walk on the Merde Side

It's a similar story with dog poo. Why should I, dog owner, waste my precious time cleaning up after my dog or taking it to poo in a place where no one will be likely to tread in it? I don't want it to poo in my living room or outside my front door, so I'll walk it a few doors away, let it dump there and then go back home and get on with my life.

Some considerate Parisian dog owners do make an effort. They take their *chiens* to pretty pedestrian streets, where the dog won't have its digestive system traumatized by the noise and vibrations of passing cars. The fact that the street cleaners don't clean up as often in the pedestrian streets isn't the dog owner's problem. On the contrary, the dog will feel more at ease and will poo quicker if there is a bit of prior doggy décor lying about.

But many dog owners prefer to go out just after the street cleaners have been through. There are dogs who need a nice clean canvas for their artwork.

These days, some dog owners do clean up after their pets, but even in posh areas, the pavements can be filthy, despite the fact that the street cleaners come by every day. Walking along the narrow pavement can be like one of those video dance games where you have to step on the panels that light up, except that in this case you try to avoid the brown panels.

When I first came to live in Paris, I used to get my shoes mired up every day. I spent my whole life with my eyes on my feet, looking like a chronically shy shoe fetishist.

I also used to take out my anger on the dog owners. I worked in a chic part of the city near the Champs-Elysées, and found it satisfying, although completely ineffectual, to tell ladies in their fur coats who were letting their poodles poop in mid-pavement, 'Il ne faut pas chier sur le trottoir, Madame' – 'You mustn't shit on the pavement, Madame.' It was fun to see them recoil in shock, but of course I hadn't taken account of the French attitude to the niceties of politeness, so instead of changing their ways, my victims simply went into a huff about my rudeness. 'Franchement,' they would gasp as little Fido dropped his muck outside a food shop. 'You Anglo-Saxons are so uncivilized.'[31]

Things got better when I learned the essential survival tactic. Or rather when I realized that my feet had evolved into Parisians. Rosie, an English friend, was over visiting from the UK for the weekend. At the end of Saturday morning she examined the soles of her trainers, compared them with mine and asked how on earth I'd kept mine so clean. I admitted I had no idea. That afternoon, as we walked, I studied my feet to see how they avoided the poop, and discovered that they'd joined forces with my eyes to beat the problem. My eyes would permanently scan the pavement about fifty yards ahead, looking for dog trouble on the horizon. If they spotted a miniature Montmartre up ahead, they alerted the feet so that when we got to the doggy mound, the feet nimbly

---

[31] To get an idea of the full effect of a well-placed *franchement*, see the Tenth Commandment on politeness.

skipped round it. Brown alert over. Rosie, meanwhile, her eyes wildly scanning the streets for signs of medieval architecture, men's backsides and clothes shops, kept on skidding. I taught her the technique I'd evidently acquired, and her feet became miraculously clean-living, especially on Sunday when the clothes shops were closed and distractions were at a minimum.

C'est la Vie

The French are a philosophical nation. They go around saying 'C'est la vie' and talking about everything's *raison d'être*. Or, more sceptically, its *je ne sais quoi*. So it's not surprising that France has produced some very influential philosophers.

There is Descartes, who is famous for 'I think therefore I am,' but whose main belief was that there was no such thing as totally reliable knowledge, a concept adopted by builders the world over when you ask them when the job is going to be finished.

And then there is Rousseau, who was born in Switzerland but did much of his philosophizing in France, and who caused all the trouble with European farm subsidies by inventing the notion of the 'noble savage' – that honest, unspoilt peasant who wouldn't even be able to conceive the existence of a fraudulent subsidy claim.

But French philosophy's greatest contribution to world thought has to be Existentialism. This is basically an intellectual justification for hating your neighbour, or at the very least denying his or her importance. It preaches that there is no morality and no absolute truth, and that life is therefore absurd and meaningless. Nothing really matters, therefore it doesn't really matter if I push in the queue in front of you.

So if you're at the restaurant and you ask the man at the next table why he is blowing smoke in your onion soup, and he replies, 'I don't know, but it doesn't matter because life is basically meaningless,' you know that you're sitting next to an Existentialist.

Amongst the most famous philosophers in the movement was Albert Camus, who wrote L'Etranger, an existential novel with a hero who cares so little about his fellow beings that he shoots one of them for no reason at all.

The biggest Existentialist star, though, was Jean-Paul Sartre, who wrote Huis Clos (translated as In Camera or No Exit), in which two women and a man are sent to hell and end up locked in a room together for eternity. They understandably get on each other's nerves, which leads Sartre to the conclusion that 'hell is other people'. If that's not a good reason to blow smoke in someone's dinner, I don't know what is.

I had a great Sartre moment on the Paris metro once. I was sitting reading a book, and I must have been jiggling about without noticing because I suddenly realized that the man next to me was furious. Our eyes met and he said, ironically, 'Ça va?' He jiggled his shoulders and elbows around to show me how I'd been annoying him, and I saw the title of the book he was trying to read – it was *Huis Clos*. My mouth opened to say 'Hell is other people, huh?', but the sound never came out. Here was one Frenchman who hated his neighbour enough already.

Phrases you might need when dealing with an inconsiderate French person

Note: you can make all of these stronger and more conflictual if you add 'merde' at the end.

Je sais que vous avez le droit de fumer, mais est-ce que vous pouvez souffler votre fumée ailleurs, s'il vous plaît?	Dje say ke voo zavay l'drwa de foomay may ess kavoo poovay sooflay votra foomay a-yeur seal voo play?	I know that you have the right to smoke, but could you please blow your smoke in a different direction?
C'est non-fumeurs ici.	Say no-foo-meurr ee-see.	This is a non-smoking area.
Pourquoi c'est moi qui fume votre cigarette?	Pork-wa say mwa ki foom votra see-garett?	Why am I smoking your cigarette?
La queue est ici.	Lacka ett ee-see.	There's a queue here.
Vous ne faites pas la queue, vous?	Voo na fet pa lacka voo?	Don't you ever queue up?
Vous êtes poli, vous	Voo et polly voo	You're very polite, aren't you?

(Say with as much irony as possible. If you're not sure of your ability to convey irony in a foreign language, laugh at the end, the only way of being sure that a French person knows an English-speaker is not being serious.)

CONTINUED...

C'est à moi, uh.	*Setta mwa, uh.*	Hey, I'm next.
	(In a shop, for example.)	

(In a shop, for example.)

J'attends depuis dix minutes, moi.	*Djaton dapwee dee minoot mwa.*	I've been waiting for ten minutes.

(If someone pushes in in front of you, it is always advisable to exaggerate the time you've been waiting.)

Vous me permettez de descendre s'il vous plaÎt?	*Voom pair mettaid day sondra, seal voo play?*	Will you allow me to get off please?

(If a train or the metro is crowded, people may try to get on before you can get off.)

Pourquoi vous roulez en moto sur le trottoir?	*Pork-wa voo roolay o moto syur le trot-wa?*	Why are you riding your motorbike on the pavement?

C'est rouge!	*Say roodj!*	The light's red!

(Here, for full effect, you can add connard *for a male driver or* connasse *for a female, but it's probably best to do so only if there's no risk that the driver will get out and attack you.)*

French waiters and waitresses sometimes adopt extreme tactics to avoid serving their customers.

THE
9TH
COMMANDMENT

Tu Ne Seras Pas Servi
THOU SHALT NOT BE SERVED

THOU SHALT NOT BE SERVED

IN FRANCE, 'SERVICE INDUSTRY' CAN OFTEN BE A CONTRADIC-TION in terms. Everyone who has been there for any length of time has stories about being ignored, sent away without getting what they want, or quite simply insulted.

And this doesn't only happen to foreigners. The French can get just as bad service as anyone else in France. The only way to get great service all the time is to be an incredibly good-looking woman. Not that I've ever tried being an incredibly good-looking woman – I don't have the knees for it. It's just that I've often watched and waited as a babe gets fawned over while I'm standing in line or sitting at a table wondering if I'm ever going to be asked what I want.

So, given that very few of us will ever be incredibly good-looking women, we may need help getting decent service.

---

[32] At the end of this chapter, you'll find a few essential French words and phrases for the linguistically challenged who would like to get served. Use those and you're in with a fighting chance.

The first thing to do is to speak French.[32] If you can't do that, you're as done for as a fat snail on a barbecue, unless you're in an obviously international place like an airport, a Paris department store or the Dordogne.

If you can speak the basic French necessary to communicate what you want, or at least know how to say that you can't speak the necessary French, then the only other thing you need to do is remember one simple rule of life in France.

It is this: ultimately, if you manage to gain the other person's attention, and convince them that your cause is worthwhile, you can get fantastic service. You will find people who bend the rules, work the system on your behalf and make a huge effort to give you the service you're after. It's only if you annoy, insult or bore them that you're in the *merde*.

Lots of French people in the service sector – all sectors, in fact – are virtually impossible to fire or reprimand, and a 15 per cent service charge is automatically added to all restaurant and café bills, so if push comes to shove, they don't give a damn whether you get good service or not. The essential thing is not to lose your temper, however strong the temptation may be. As long as you view the whole French service experience as a game, it will become a learning process. If it ended in *merde* this time, next time you'll do better.

The Waiter Can't Wait

The French waiter is a much misunderstood creature. A bit like the hyena. The hyena isn't really laughing at you – it just naturally makes a smug-sounding noise. French waiters are sometimes the same. They can also be incredibly charming, helpful and efficient. As can the hyena, when feeding hunks of dismembered antelope to its young.

The trick is not to present yourself as a potential antelope. If the waiter is in a rush or a bad mood, or both, you may get mauled. You must always remember that you are a lion, and give the impression that you know the savannah as well as the waiter, even if you don't. This doesn't mean that you have to be a wine buff (though knowing the difference between champagne and Chablis can help) – that's where the waiter can be legitimately asked for advice, and will be glad to give it. What it means is that as you sit there in your café or restaurant seat, you should feel as at ease as anyone else in the place.

If for any reason you don't feel at ease – if you're being pointedly ignored by the waiting staff, which can happen – just do what a lion does if it decides that its resting place isn't shady enough – cheerfully and calmly get up and leave. As long, of course, as this isn't the only eating place you've seen open for the last twenty kilometres, in which case you just have to tell yourself 'C'*est la vie*' and get on with it.

And rest assured, if you do bite the bullet and pull off

the whole ordering trick, then you will gain the respect of all but the most awkward of French waiters or waitresses, and get as good service as they are capable of giving.

How to Get Good Service in France

What I've learnt in twelve years of living in France is that getting good service here is anything but a divine right. It's like a computer game. You've got to press the right buttons or it'll be game over before you've had a chance to buy a single croissant.

And before play even starts, you've got to realize that your opponent, the French person offering service, is not your friend. I've been served in California by people who seemed to be offering me their body when all I'd ordered was a glass of seaweed and echinacea juice. You won't get that in France, unless of course you happen to stumble into a massage parlour that also offers health drinks. But then again, you probably don't want the French waiter as your friend, so what do you care whether he likes you or not? The important thing is that he should respect you as a worthy adversary, not want you as a *pétanque* partner.

If you bear this in mind, you won't be put off as you try to progress through the three levels of the French service game.

Level One
IGNORE THE CUSTOMER

My worst experience of this was when I tried to get a cup of coffee at a certain trendy café near the Centre Pompidou. The décor was designed by Philippe Starck and the prices suggested that they were still trying to pay off the furnishings. The round metal tables were welded to the floor, which really ought to have warned me that the basic attitude to the customers here was that they were potential furniture thieves.

The place wasn't very busy, and there were only three occupied tables up on the mezzanine. I sat in a steel armchair and waited to be served. Sure enough, after ten minutes or so, a waiter ambled up the stairs, a very tall male-model type in a black suit.

As you should always do with a French waiter, I looked him straight in the eye. As soon as he blinks in your direction, you have to blurt out your order before he can get away. In this case, though, he met my gaze, pouted moodily as if I was a *Vogue* photographer snapping him on the catwalk, and turned his back on me. He took the orders at the other tables, ambled back towards me, and, avoiding eye contact this time, went downstairs.

What did I do wrong?, I wondered. Had I forgotten that I was wearing my invisibility cloak?

In fact, I think I made two fatal errors.

First, I hesitated for that millisecond when I had his attention. I let myself be beaten into submission by his withering look. I ought to have got out my 'Bonjour, un café, s'il vous plaît' in that minuscule window of opportunity between stare and pout.

Second, I now suspect that I was on the wrong side of an invisible border. I wasn't at one of 'his' tables. If this was the case, the other waiter was obviously excused stairs that day (fell off a catwalk, maybe?), because no one else made any attempt to serve on the mezzanine. And my waiter certainly couldn't be bothered to explain the situation to me.

Whatever. This kind of thing will happen to Parisians and visitors alike. It's a trendy jungle out there sometimes. It's not worth worrying about. The only solution is to laugh and leave. There are enough cafés in Paris where you can actually get served.

That was an extreme example, of course. You're much more likely to come across shop assistants who carry on gossiping about their boss as you wait to be served. In that case, if you really need what they have on offer, you should interrupt the conversation with a cheery but insistent 'bonjour!', which is French for 'Are you going to serve me or what?'

The key thing is not to get annoyed. And this is going to be especially important when you reach . . .

Level Two
JUST SAY NON

In France, when a girl says no she often means yes. So does a guy, for that matter. I'm not saying that they want to get raped. Though sometimes getting good service in France does feel a bit like non-consensual sex.

Here's how the French 'no means yes' works.

I was in Reims to visit the champagne cellars, and didn't want to leave the city without seeing the most spectacular of them, at the Pommery winery. Only trouble was, it was Sunday lunchtime, I was due to leave on the five o'clock train, and you have to book a place on a guided tour.

I phoned Pommery and asked when the next tour was.

'Oh, we haven't got any vacancies till the four forty-five tour,' the hostess told me.

'You've got nothing at all before that?'

'No, sorry. We're completely booked up.'

At this point, the faint-hearted customer is supposed to ring off and leave the hostess in peace with her neat reservation list. But I've played the game before.

'My train's at five,' I said, 'so four forty-five would be too late.'

'OK,' the hostess replied, 'how about two thirty?'

'Perfect,' I said, and reserved.

There was absolutely no point entering into an abstract moral discussion about why the hell she hadn't offered two thirty in the first place. I'd got what I wanted, so who cared?

This happened to me again more recently, and I must be getting even better at the game because the result was an even more astonishing success.

I was travelling from Lannion in Brittany to Paris, first taking a regional train and then changing on to the mainline TGV at Saint Brieuc. It was February 6th.

At Lannion, I stamped my ticket in the *composteur* machine and got on my regional train, only for the ticket inspector, the *contrôleur*, to tell me that the date on my ticket was wrong. It said February 10th instead of 6th. This, I knew, wasn't really my fault, because I'd told the man at the Gare de Lyon when booking my ticket that I wanted to come back on the Monday, and he'd got the date wrong. But there was no point telling the *contrôleur* this, because he'd only have told me that it was my fault for not checking the date. Which was true, I suppose.

'It's no problem on this train, because it's a non-reservation service, but you'll have to change your ticket before you get on the TGV, which is reservation-only. You can do it at Saint Brieuc station,' he said, a worrying prospect given that I had only fifteen minutes to find the ticket office, queue up, get the change made and catch my connecting train.

I was first out the doors of the regional train in Saint Brieuc, dashed to the ticket office, and found only three or four people ahead of me in the queue, which was an organized line with barriers, and not some anarchic ruck as it would have been a few years ago. Things were looking promising.

My turn came – still ten minutes to go – and I set out

to explain my problem to the lady behind the counter, a youngish woman who looked fairly at ease with the world and not out to prove to her customers what a cruel place it can be. Which was a relief.

'*Bonjour*,' I said brightly, as always.

'*Bonjour*,' she replied, a little too suspiciously for my liking.

So, taking a lesson from the (as yet unwritten) first chapter of this book, I heaped the blame on myself.

'I made a mistake when booking my ticket. I got one for *dix février* instead of *six février*,' I said. I handed it to her. She read – rather slowly, I thought – my itinerary. The regional train's times of departure and arrival, the same for the TGV, with my seat and carriage number, and the wrong date.

'I can't change a ticket once you've started the journey,' she finally replied.

'But I haven't started the TGV bit of the journey.'

'Yes, but you've *composted* your ticket. I can't replace it.'

This, I knew, was the *moment critique*. She had pursed her lips and put the ticket down in front of her, as if to wash her hands of it. If I gave up now and picked up the ticket, I was a goner.

'Yes, I *composted* it before I got on the train at Lannion,' I said, pushing the ticket barely a millimetre back towards her across the counter, 'because I didn't know it was the wrong date. It was the *contrôleur* who noticed.'

'You should have checked the date when you bought the ticket.'

'Yes, you are right, but I just assumed that the ticket

seller would give me the right date. I don't understand how the mistake happened. I always knew I was coming back today. Perhaps I said *"dix"* instead of *"six"*.'

We'd reached an impasse. But we'd had a nice philosophical discussion about the nature of my mistake and the way the French railway ticketing system works. And the most important thing was that I had found a comeback – a non-aggressive reply – to everything she said. I clearly wasn't going to give up and go away, or offer to buy a new ticket.

'I'll see what I can do,' she said, and went away with my ticket.

I felt like the accused waiting for the jury to return its verdict. The SNCF clock on the wall clicked one more minute, two. My TGV was out there somewhere, heading towards me. Less than eight minutes to go. Maybe, I thought, it was a war of attrition. I was meant to panic and rush off to the platform, get on the train without a ticket and pay a fine.

Another click passed and she came back. Her lips were still pursed, but she looked me in the eye, just like the jurors do when they're going to find you not guilty. A wave of joy swept over me. I wasn't going to the guillotine after all.

'OK, I'll change it,' she said. 'But this is totally exceptional. Don't do it again.'

'Ah, *c'est super, merci*,' I said. 'I really don't know how it happened.'

She slowly wrote something on the ticket in red ink, presumably her reasons for agreeing to this exceptional exchange. Another minute clicked by, but I kept my mouth shut. She was in control now, she knew when the train was due in, she would get the job done in time.

'Give me your credit card,' she said. I hesitated for a moment, wondering why. 'I have to credit you with ten euros,' she added, 'because this new ticket is less expensive.'

'Oh.' I handed over the credit card, and watched her print out a new Saint Brieuc–Paris ticket and a credit-card refund slip for ten euros.

'I've reimbursed the full price of your original ticket and issued a new one for just the Saint Brieuc–Paris leg. It was the only way to do it,' she said. 'Voilà.'

She handed over my double prize. My honest mistake had earned me ten euros.

'C'est très gentil,' I said. 'Merci beaucoup.' I wished her a bonne semaine (good week) and rushed off to get my TGV.

I wondered why she'd done this for me. No doubt my innocent mistake and my apologetic nature had counted in my favour. And my tacit refusal to give in and accept my fate had been a key factor, too.

On top of this, I'm sure that the woman got a kick out of the knowledge that she held my fate in her hands. Her decision would affect my journey and my mood. She had the power to make or break my day. And, like most French counter assistants I have met, she used her power benevolently. They only take the opportunity to annoy you if they dislike you personally, so it's best not to give them the chance. Play the lost innocent, stay polite and apologetic, and they'll take pity on you. Tell them that their system is absurd, though, and they'll use all its absurd power against you.

Again, as at the Pommery cellar, the vital thing was not to get annoyed at the initial 'no' in response to my request, a feat that becomes almost impossible when you reach . . .

Level Three
TRY TO DRIVE THE CUSTOMER MAD

The most frequent examples of this happen when there are two or more people serving at the same time, in a tourist office, bank, car-hire place or shop.

One customer inadvertently causes a problem. Let's say someone wants to do an unusual transaction at the bank. Approximately three seconds after the problem has arisen, all the counter assistants have stopped serving their customers and are gathered at the window where the non-standard-transaction dilemma has cropped up.

I've lost out at this stage of the game many times in the past, and almost always because I rose to the bait too soon, or misjudged the placing of the moral onus (which can be as painful as it sounds). The worst case of misplaced onus that I have suffered in France was when my mobile phone wouldn't recharge, and I took it into the local phone shop for a diagnosis.

There were three sales people on duty, and no obvious queuing system – it was first come, first served, but only if you stuck up for yourself. All three sales assistants were busy, and there was one person in front of me.

One of the assistants was annoying me intensely by discussing her customer's scarf – 'Elle est belle, where did you get it?', 'It was made by a friend of mine', 'Oh, yes, does she sell them?', 'No, but she ought to, don't you think?', 'Yes, and if she decides to go into business, let me know, won't you?'. Nyaarrgh.

But it was no use wading in and asking whether one customer's scarf was more important to the phone shop than another customer's phone. Truth be told, I was a bit scared of the answer I'd get. Anyway, after a couple of minutes, two of the assistants – including the potential scarf-buyer – miraculously became free at the same time.

One of them asked how he could help the man ahead of me, who said he wanted to take out a new subscription. Scarf Woman half-turned to me, her service-giver's automatic smile on her face. But as she did so, she glanced across at the man who wanted the subscription, and then, as I stepped forward with phone out-thrust, she suddenly veered away from me and joined the two men in front of a computer. I couldn't believe it. I didn't even exist.

For a few seconds I stood there watching the three of them bending over the screen as if it was showing the next day's lottery results. If the scarf affair hadn't already annoyed me, I might have waited a couple more minutes to judge the situation, but I let my frustration out.

'Excuse me interrupting,' I said with as much fake politeness as I could muster, 'but does it really need two of you to deal with one person?'

'Yes, it does, actually,' Scarf Woman told me sternly. 'My colleague is a trainee and needs help with new accounts.'

'Ah, sorry,' I said, thinking 'Oh *merde*, I've had it now.'

In a way it wasn't my fault. A good sales person would have told me that she'd get to me as soon as she'd helped out her trainee. But that was now irrelevant. I knew I'd just wasted even more minutes of my life. All three of the sales people had heard the exchange, and none of them were going to hurry up and serve me. The man opening an account even had a homemade-looking scarf. The woman was probably going to ask him to write out the knitting pattern.

Ten full minutes later, Madame Scarf dragged herself away from the trainee and grudgingly served me. I explained my problem. She took the phone, tested it and told me that my recharge lead was probably faulty, and here was a new one. Twenty-eight euros, please.

As I paid, I looked into the recharge socket of the phone, and noticed something I hadn't seen before.

'Should that little shiny thing be in there?' I asked.

'Yes,' she said, giving me my change, wishing me a tetchy '*bonne journée*' and turning to the nearest fluffy-neckwear-owning customer.

When I got home, instead of taking the lead out of its wrapping, I got some tweezers, poked about in the recharge socket, and pulled out a little piece of aluminium foil that had got in there, probably from a chewing-gum wrapper in my pocket. I plugged in my old recharge cable and the phone instantly began to charge up.

Oh, double *merde*, I thought. If I hadn't caused a scene

at the shop I could go back, play the stupid innocent and get a refund. But now I'm stuffed. It would be, 'Oh, well, that's not our problem, you should have checked,' etc, etc.

I still have that lead unopened in its packet, and am patiently waiting for someone to say that they want a new Sagem recharge cable for their birthday. And all because I let myself be provoked by a typical French service situation.

I don't want to suggest that service in France is always bad. It's just that getting good service is often an effort. But that is what makes it so rewarding, too. You come across such great professionals. French shops, for instance, can be temples of good service. After all, this is still a nation of individual shopkeepers, so you can buy your stuffed olives, perfume, fish or lingerie from an expert. But the greatest service professionals have to be the ones with the worst reputation – waiters. Until you've been served by a *good* French waiter, you've never been served at all.

I once had lunch at the Jules Verne restaurant up on the Eiffel Tower. There I was, with one of the most beautiful restaurant views in the world spread out below me, being allowed to enjoy it by waiters who didn't force me to spend half the meal scanning the kitchen door for signs of life. The service was swift and polite, and the waiter practically knew the name of every cow, sheep or goat that had provided the cheese on the trolley.

It was pure class, like playing a game with a champion and getting treated as an equal. Which is the bottom line of French service. In France, they have a saying – *'le client est roi'*, or the customer is king. But this is total nonsense, because you, the customer, are at very best an equal.

And if you're tempted to get uppity and insist that you're a *roi*, just remember what France did to its royal family.

Mots Magiques

Even if you've got the right attitude, you need the appropriate vocabulary to turn getting served in a French café from a chore into a *plaisir*. Here are a few magic words:

GARÇON ('GARSO')

First, one to forget. No *one* shouts '*Garçon!*' in a French café. Unless they don't want to get served, that is. To attract a waiter or waitress's attention, just raise your arm and call out '*S'il vous plaît!*', or catch their eye and say '*Bonjour*' (or '*Bonsoir*' if it's the evening, of course). Remember that in the French service sector, saying '*Bonjour*' and '*Bonsoir*' is the accepted code for 'Hello, I'm sorry to interrupt your phone call/racing results/nail-varnishing/cigarette/chat with your friend, etc, but I would like to be served eventually if it's not too much trouble.'

EXPRESS ('EXPRESS')

If you like your espresso, this is what to order. You can ask for *un café noir*, or just *un petit café*, but *un express* is what the waiters themselves call it. Use this word and they'll think, 'Aha, this person has been in a French café before, no point trying to rip him/her off.'

ALLONGÉ ('ALLON-DJAY')

Café allongé is the waiters' name for an *express* with extra water. It's weaker than an espresso but less like bison pee than American coffee.

CRÈME ('KREM')

Waiters' jargon for a *café au lait*. All too often I hear English-speaking tourists asking for 'un café olé si voo play' and I know they're going to end up with a cripplingly expensive tureen of beige soup. For full effect, make sure you get the pronunciation right – 'krremm'. Imagine trying to say it while dislodging an oyster that has got stuck on your tonsils.

NOISETTE ('NWA-ZET')

If you want an espresso with a dash of milk, this is what to ask for. It's short for *un café noisette*, or hazelnut-coloured coffee. But of course you knew that.

DÉCA ('DAY-KA')

This is the waiters' word for a decaf. Useful if you're planning to get any sleep after a heavy dinner.

THÉ AU LAIT ('TAYOLAY')

If you want a drink approaching English-style tea, you must remember to ask for *thé au lait*, or you will probably just get a small teapot of hot water with the tea bag, still in its packet, lying on your saucer. Ask for *thé au lait* and you will also get a tiny jug of milk. Even so, unless the café does Earl Grey or Darjeeling, the warm liquid you receive will probably remind you of the description of Arthur Dent's computer-generated drink in *The Hitchhiker's Guide to the Galaxy* – 'almost, but not quite, entirely unlike tea'.

DEMI ('D'MEE')

Ordering a beer is just as tricky as getting coffee or tea. The standard measure in France is *un demi*, literally a half. This is not a half litre (come on, you can't expect the French to make things *that* simple). It's twenty-five centilitres, about half a pint. Serving beer is the waiter's favourite way of ripping off tourists. In summer, the Champs-Elysées is lined with foreign visitors forlornly trying to finish the two-litre flagons of lager they received when they rashly asked for 'oon beer sivoo play'. Some waiters are so determined to make an extra euro or two that even if you ask for a *demi* they might come back with '*Petit, moyen ou grand?*' (Small, medium or large?). The required response is a look of bafflement and the killer phrase '*Mais un demi est un demi, non?*'

PRESSION ('PRESSYO')

Draught beer. If you manage to get the *demi* business right, the waiter might still try to trick you by rattling off the names of different beers at Thierry Henry speed. Get it wrong and you'll end up with an expensive bottle. If you say '*un demi pression*' you can look over at the beer taps and read or point. At worst you'll end up with the slightly more expensive of the two or three brands on sale. A couple of tips – a *seize* is a relatively cheap '1664', and Heineken is pronounced 'eh-neck-EN'.

QUART ('KAR')

You can almost always get a *pichet* ('pee-shay') of wine instead of a (more expensive) bottle or half-bottle. On the menus the *pichets* will often be marked as '25cl' and '50cl', or a quarter-litre/half-litre. You can sound really experienced in restaurant-survival techniques if you ask for *'un quart de rouge'* or *'un pichet de cinquante de rouge'*. Remember that a bottle (75 centilitres) is six glasses, so a *quart* is two, and 50cl is four.

CARAFE ('KARAF')

Only the snootiest of restaurants will refuse to serve you tap water. But you've got to ask for *'une carafe d'eau'*, a small jug of water. Failure to specify this will result in you receiving a bottle of Evian, San Pellegrino or Badoit, which is not unpleasant, just more expensive. If you want to be really clever, when a waiter or waitress offers you branded water, just say no thanks and ask for 'Château Chirac', meaning a carafe of normal French tap water. The risk here is that the waiter will think you're too clever for your own good and might plan some form of comeuppance like 'forgetting' to bring you bread.

MARCEL MARCEAU ('   ')

The French have long forgotten who Marcel Marceau is, but his legacy lives on. So when you want to pay, there's no need to call the waiter or waitress over to your table and explain this. You simply catch his or her eye and mime writing something on a notebook, while mouthing *'l'addition'* (the bill, pronounced 'addi-sio').

This means, I want to pay. Or you can just hold up your credit card with a willing look on your face. This will bring the waiter over with a little credit-card machine. Surely this is the biggest advantage of the chip and pin system – no more chasing waiters when they disappear into a back room to email your credit-card details to a crime syndicate. In France, they'll usually come over and let you type in your pin number. And they'll even look away while you do it.

Phrases you must understand if you don't want to annoy a French waiter

(and what the waiter really means)

Vous avez fait votre choix?	Voozavay fay vot shwa?	Have you made your choice?

(You've been sitting there with the menu long enough, and this is a restaurant, not a dentist's waiting room.)

. . . .

Ça a été? *or* Ça s'est bien passé?	Sa-ah ay-tay *or* Sassay bya passay?	How was it?

(Don't forget the tip. Especially if you're about to pay by credit card, as there's usually no space for tips on French credit-card slips.)

. . . .

Je voudrais encaisser *or* Je peux vous encaisser?	Dje voodray o'kessay *or* Dje peu voozo kessay?	I would like to cash up *or* Can you pay me?

(I've finished my shift, so be quick about it, and don't forget to tell me to keep the change because I won't be coming back to your table to pick up any tip you might leave.)

. . . .

Le service est compris.	L'sair-veece ay compree.	Service is included (*the footnote on your bill*).

(OK, so there's a 15 per cent service charge included in the price but I expect a tip, otherwise don't bother coming here again.)

Some practical training in the French service attitude

Read the following short exchanges and decide which approach you need to adopt in order to get good service in France.

(A hint: if you choose any of conversations one to four, you might be better off either re-reading this chapter or not bothering to come to France.)

CONVERSATION 1

Customer: Bonjour, can I *(fill in slightly complex administrative or service request)* here?
French service provider: No, you can't.
Customer: Oh, *au revoir*.

. . . .

CONVERSATION 2

Customer: Bonjour, can I *(fill in, etc)* here?
French service provider: No, you can't.
Customer: But *(fill in competitor's name)* does it.
French service provider: Well, go there then. Au *revoir*.

. . . .

CONVERSATION 3

Customer: Bonjour, can I *(fill in, etc)* here?
French service provider: No, you can't.
Customer: But that is totally absurd. That's not how we do things in *(fill in the name of your country)*.
French service provider: Well, I can only suggest you go back there then. *Bon voyage*.

CONTINUED...➤

CONVERSATION 4

Customer: *Bonjour*, can I (*fill in, etc*) here?
French service provider: No, you can't.
Customer: But that is totally absurd! Why don't you (*fill in perfectly logical and simple way of changing the system so that it would be possible to do what you want*)?
French service provider: It's not my fault, I didn't invent the system. *Au revoir*.

. . . .

CONVERSATION 5

Customer: *Bonjour*, can I (*fill in, etc*) here?
French service provider: No, you can't.
Customer: Ah (*fill in look of despair*). I was really hoping you could do it (*fill in more philosophical but still basically despairing look*). I don't know where else to try.
French service provider: Have you tried (*fill in competitor or other department*)?
Customer: Yes, they said I should try you.
French service provider: Ah. (*Allow a few moments of silent contemplation during which you do not budge an inch from the counter.*)
Customer: I don't know what to do. Can't you help me?
French service provider: OK, I'm not supposed to do this, but . . . (*fill in service provider doing exactly what you wanted them to, but feeling as if they decided to do it, rather than having to accept that it's their job to serve you so they were obliged to do it anyway*).

. . . .

Admittedly, Conversation 5 is truncated, and might require a bit more persistence, but as long as you don't show any signs of weakening or irritation, you should get the service you want.

Bonne chance!

Things you must be able to say if you can't speak French and still hope to get good service

Désolé, je ne parle pas français.	*Day-zolay, dje n' parl pa fro-say.*	Sorry, I can't speak French.

(This is much better than asking 'Parlez-vous anglais?' which might oblige the French service person to admit that no, they can't, which will make them feel inadequate or nationalistic or both, and ensure that you get the worst service possible.)

Vous parlez très bien anglais.	*Voo parlay tray byen ong-lay.*	You speak very good English.

(Even if they can't, tell them they can. They will feel good about themselves, and therefore give better service. Unless, of course, their English is so abysmal that they think you're being sarcastic. So on second thoughts, use this with discretion — in extreme circumstances, an admiring 'ah, vous parlez anglais' might be praise enough.)

Nous les Anglo-Saxons, nous sommes nuls en langues.	*Noo laze onglo-saxo noo som nool o' lon-ga.*	We Anglo-Saxons are rubbish at languages.

(This admission of ignorance will probably go down so well that the French person will say no, we French are even worse, and give you wonderful service out of a kind of linguistic guilt.)

CONTINUED...➤

Je ne comprends pas comment c'est arrivé, mais...	*Dje neu com-pro pa komm-o set a-reevay, may...*	I don't know how this happened, but...

(*If you admit ignorance, they know you're not going to blame them, so you get off on the right foot. France was the country that invented the concept of human rights, so they are also suckers when it comes to admissions of helplessness.*)

J'ai un petit problème.	*Djay uh p'tee prob-lemm.*	I have a small problem.

(*If they know it's not a big problem, and therefore not liable to spill over into their lunch hour, they'll be more likely to help you out.*)

Pouvez-vous m'aider?	*Poovay voo may-day?*	Can you help me?

(*Throw yourselves on their mercy. The French enjoy thinking up ways of helping people, especially if it gives them the chance to bend the rules and annoy their boss.*)

'Hands above the waist, s'il vous plaît, Marcel.' Jean-Philippe (right)
gives etiquette lessons to new residents of Paris's arty Latin Quarter.

THE
10TH
COMMANDMENT

Tu Seras Poli
THOU SHALT BE POLITE
(and simultaneously rude)

THOU SHALT BE POLITE
(and simultaneously rude)

THE FRENCH ARE GENIUSES AT BEING POLITE WHILE SIMUL-
taneously insulting you. You've never been put
down until you've been put down by a Frenchman. And
they do it with such aplomb. They can wish you a good
day, call you an idiot and send you sprawling into the
verbal gutter before you can even open your mouth to
reply.

I was once queuing at a famous French restaurant that
doesn't take reservations because it doesn't need to. A
chic-looking American expat, with a smug 'yes I live here'
look on his face, sidled to the front of the line and quietly
informed the maître d' that he'd reserved a table for two.

'Reserved a table, Monsieur?' the maître d' replied for
the whole queue to hear. 'We don't take reservations. Is
Monsieur sure he didn't call the McDonald's on the corner
by mistake?'

He got a big laugh, and presumably lost a customer
for life, but couldn't resist the temptation to get in an
insult that put the pretentious interloper firmly in his

place. The French may claim to live in a classless republic, but they are very keen on keeping everyone in their place. And politeness, combined with extreme rudeness, is often the best way to do it.

Before they insult you, though, you will see nothing but impeccable manners. At a time when English-speakers all introduce each other by their first names, the French still call one another Monsieur or Madame. One way to attract the attention of a waiter or an evasive sales assistant is to call out 'Monsieur!' Yes, the customer is having to say 'sir' to get served. The world can be turned on its head once the French start using their politeness on you.

A Bad Début

One Saturday morning, at a slightly snooty cheese shop near my home in Paris, I saw a woman get sadistically put in her place by a man in a white overall.

I was being attended to by the female half of the husband-and-wife *crémerie* team, and was ogling some small decorative goat's cheeses – a selection of round pats of fresh white cheese sprinkled with black pepper, encrusted in sultanas or coated with herbs. But the viciousness of the snub was shocking enough to distract me from my drooling.

The victim, a middle-aged lady, bustled into the shop, already rifling through her handbag for her purse. Probably in a rush to get home to give her kids their lunch.

'Un *litre de lait frais demi-écrémé, s'il vous plaît*,' she said. A bottle of semi-skimmed milk.

The male co-owner exchanged a look with his wife, who raised her eyebrows in sympathy. '*Bonjour*,' he said to the woman.

'Un *litre de lait frais demi-écrémé, s'il vous plaît*,' she repeated, getting out her cash.

'*Bonjour*,' the owner repeated, a little louder this time.

'*Je voudrais juste un litre de lait*,' she said, changing tack and still not fully realizing that there was a problem. She was explaining that she only wanted milk, and was not splurging on the expensive cheeses, because cheese-shop owners sometimes think that it is beneath their dignity to sell unfermented dairy products, especially semi-skimmed ones.

'Don't you ever wish people a good day, Madame?' the cheese seller asked. Subtext: I am not a servant, I am a noble purveyor of fine foods, I have a house in the country and a cleaning lady who irons my overalls, so you're not getting your piffling bottle of milk until you say hello.

'Oh, sorry, yes, of course, *bonjour*,' the woman said, blushing and apologizing. She looked expectantly across at the cheese seller. She was still in a hurry, still hoping to buy some milk and get back home before the weekend was over.

'*Bonjour, Madame*,' the cheese man said. 'What would you like?'

The customer had to repeat her request for a bottle of milk, and then wait while the shopkeeper counted out her change and put the plastic bottle in a bag, 'because we like to treat our customers *comme il faut*'. He saw absolutely no contradiction between what he was doing and what he was saying.

At last the woman was allowed to leave the shop, with a loud '*au revoir*' from both husband and wife ringing in her reddened ears.

I really should have walked out, but I'd been sent on a last-minute errand to get the cheese for a lunch party, so I meekly made my selection, paid, and wished them a polite '*bonne journée*'.

By the way, I must emphasize a key aspect of the previous scene – it was a clash between two French people. We non-French people often think that the French are trying to insult us because we're foreign, but it's not true. They're like that with each other, too.

Coming Through, with a Pout

The French are experts with their elbows. Sometimes, walking along a pavement or trying to shop in a crowded supermarket, you might think they were all educated at an American football university. However, they must be the only people on earth capable of shoving you unceremoniously out of the way with perfect manners. And all because of one word: *pardon*. In theory, you are meant to say '*pardon*' (pronounced 'pardo', ending with a pout) *before* shoving anyone or instead of doing so, but in practice you say it as you shove.

In Paris, the pavements can get very narrow, and are often partially blocked by empty rubbish bins and the little metal posts that physically prevent drivers from parking on the pavement (it's the only way to stop them, short of minefields). Anyway, you often have to weave in and out of obstacles as you walk. This may involve waiting while someone else squeezes between, say, a wheelie bin and a shop window. In which case, they're supposed to, and often do, say *'pardon'*. Some people, though, simply blunder forwards mumbling *'pardon, pardon'* for form's sake and not worrying if they have to crush a few toes or force someone out into the road. They've respected the convention, so everything is all right.

This is not a totally risk-free strategy. An overt blunderer might come up against someone who retaliates with a scathing reminder of the need to do things *comme il faut*. A person who has been shoved, or, if they are very good at retaliation, who is about to be shoved, may express their disapproval with another key word: *franchement*. This, pronounced 'frONsh-ma', is a lot like the English 'honestly', but is usually said with a look of such crushing scorn – shared if possible with everyone else within ten yards – that you're transported back to the seventeenth century, and it feels as if someone has just farted in the presence of the Sun King. *Franchement*, such a person does not belong in Paris. They should be banished to some barbarous wilderness like Brittany or America . . .

To Kiss or Not to Kiss?

The range of polite French words and gestures is huge. At the Parisian company where I used to work, a trip down to the coffee machines on the ground floor was more socially complex than taking tea with a Samurai.

If you encountered someone in the corridor or the lift, first of all you had to decide whether you'd seen them before.

If you hadn't, you would say *'bonjour'* anyway, because France is a polite country. If you *had* seen them before, they were either a *'bonjour'* acquaintance (that is, people you know but not all that well), or you were on more familiar *'salut'* ('hi') terms.[33]

In either case, two men would have to shake hands. Women were more complicated (as is often the case in France).

If there was a woman involved in the encounter, cheek-kissing might or might not be necessary. *'Salut'* women would always expect a kiss. *'Bonjour'* women might not, but then they might not expect a handshake either. Shaking the hand of a woman you know can feel a bit butch. I would often meet my immediate boss, a woman, walking with one or two of the (male) directors. I would shake the directors' hands, saying *'salut, Jacques'* to one of them (because he was a 'hi' kind of director),

....

[33] *Salut* is a wonderful word, because it can also be used to say good-bye. Though care should be taken when pronouncing it ('saloo') so as not to confuse it with *salaud* ('salo'), meaning bastard.

and '*bonjour, Monsieur*' to another (whom I knew less well). I would say '*salut*' to my boss, but not shake her hand because I knew her too well to do that but not well enough to kiss her.

Sometimes it was easier to duck into the nearest office, shake the hand of the bemused occupant, and wait until the directors and my boss had gone.

Most of the above also applies when bumping into neighbours or acquaintances in the street. You have to put everyone you meet into a category – handshake, kiss, '*bonjour*' or ignore. If you have a meeting with some-one – a bank manager, estate agent, or even a doctor – it is polite to shake hands. If your estate agent starts kissing you, you know you're in trouble.

When meeting someone for the first time, the good news is that the French really do say '*enchanté*'. It feels beautifully old-fashioned to tell someone you're enchanted to meet them, especially if you really are. Looking into someone's eyes and telling them they're enchanting is so much more exciting than a quick 'hi, how ya doin?' And if you're *not* enchanted to meet them, it feels deliciously hypocritical to tell them you are. It's a no-lose situation.

The big question when meeting a woman for the first time is, kiss or no kiss? Some men chicken out of this by only kissing women they fancy, or women whom they have to kiss if they don't want to annoy someone (e.g. their girlfriend's best friend or sister). The general rule for a man meeting a woman, or a woman meeting any-one, is this: if the other person is a friend of a friend, close relative of a friend, under the age of thirty, at a party of any kind, someone you might like to kiss more amply later on, or just looks as if they're expecting a kiss, you have to kiss them or they'll think you're a cold, unfriendly Anglo-Saxon.

If you think you've made the wrong decision and missed a kiss, you can always put things right by kissing when you say goodbye, which is a friendly way of saying that now you know each other better, it's OK to get politely physical.

What Do I Do with My Lips?

If you do want to kiss, there is a definite technique to it.

In Paris, cheek-kissing, or *faire la bise*, involves two 'mwas' with little or no actual lip–cheek contact but an audible smack of the lips. Left cheeks first, then right.[34] The no-lip-contact rule is important unless you are very closely acquainted. Someone you don't know all that well may not think that your relationship extends to smearing your bodily fluids on their face – the complete opposite of a 'French kiss', in fact.

Even teenagers manage to control themselves in this respect. Boys will brush cheeks with girls in a way that seems to negate the presence of any hormones in their bloodstream at all. These same teenage boys often

....

[34] If the two people about to kiss are wearing glasses, it is polite for the man to take his off, to avoid an embarrassing clash of frames.

shake each other's hands like old men, unless they're trying to be cool and do the rapper's hand-slapping and fist-touching thing. (Most French boys like to think they were born in the Bronx.)

Men kiss each other pretty rarely, outside of gay districts, family reunions and artists' soirées. As a male, one of the dangers of being accepted as a member of a French family is that you may be required to rub cheeks with the clan's male members. [35]

If you do get on kissing terms, you have to hope that there aren't too many unshaven men in the family. Since coming to live in France, I have developed great admiration for women with unshaven partners, who have to put up with this hairy scraping every day of their lives.

Outside Paris, by the way, the kissing ritual can vary. '*En province*', as the Parisians condescendingly call anywhere not within about a hundred kilometres of the Eiffel Tower, people often give four kisses. The Parisians say this is because their life is so dull that they have to find ways to fill the time.

To conclude: imagine if you can the following scene. It's eleven a.m. in an office building out in the four-kiss zone. Two groups of three female workers meet in the corridor on their way to a coffee machine. By the time they've finished kissing each other, it's lunchtime.

Which brings me to the next complication . . .

. . . .

[35] That sounds unfortunate. By 'rub cheeks with male members', I mean kiss the male relatives of your French girlfriend, of course, and not their genitals. Even in France that would be excessive.

Bon Bons

Even after the business of kissing and shaking hands has been dealt with, you are by no means out of the *forêt*. When you part company, don't think you can get away with *'au revoir'*. That would be much too easy. If you know people well and they're below, say, fifty, you can say *'salut'* both as hello and goodbye. But that's not enough – you also have to remember what time it is. As you part company, you have to wish the other person a good whatever period of the day it is.

At the start of the day you can wish them *'bonne journée'* (have a good day), or *'bonne matinée'* (have a good morning). Later on in the morning, *'bonne journée'* will still be OK, but a *'bonne fin de matinée'* (have a good end of the morning) is optional. If it is just before lunch, then *'bon appétit'* is of course obligatory.

After lunch, everyone must be wished *'bonne après-midi'* (have a good afternoon). Later on in the afternoon, at some hazy time around dusk, you have to start greeting people with *'bonsoir'* instead of *'bonjour'*, and leaving them with a *'bonne fin d'après midi'* or *'bonne fin de journée'*. And if you're at work and it's just before going-home time, a *'bonne soirée'* (have a good evening) will be appreciated.

The politeness game is even more varied outside the office.

Some cafés now get their staff to say *'bonne dégustation'*, literally 'good tasting'. And it is common to wish someone happiness whatever they're doing, from *'bon ski'*, *'bon film'* and *'bonne promenade'* (have a nice walk) to semi-absurd things like *'bon coiffeur'* (have a good time at the hairdresser's).

One of my favourites is *'bonne continuation'*, a formal way of wishing someone luck and happiness with whatever they're up to when you leave them. A taxi driver might say it, or someone you've been talking to on the bus. I've often wished I could walk in accidentally on two people making love, just so that I could discreetly close the door again, leaving them with a polite *'bonne continuation'*.

When you're out in the evening, the whole Japanese-tea-ceremony side of French life comes into play again. Anyone you meet will need a *'bonsoir'* (unless you're on *'salut'* terms, of course), and if you part company, they'll need a *'bonne soirée'*.

When saying goodbye after an aperitif, restaurant, film or some other event that might not be the end of the *'soirée'*, people usually wish each other *'bonne fin de soirée'*. It is quite chic to do this late on in the evening because it implies that you, and the recipient of the farewell, are night owls and probably off to some late-night champagne celebration.

It's important to bear in mind that anyone saying *'bonne nuit'* (goodnight) before they are actually heading towards their bedroom will be laughed at. Though after a day of remembering how to greet people, you might feel that bedtime can't come soon enough.

What's the Délai?

In France, a woman can – or rather should – be late for any kind of rendezvous, otherwise the man will think that she's too easy. It also avoids the embarrassment of turning up on time and seeing that the man is late. These days it is usual for a man to send a text message saying that he'll be a few minutes late. This is not only polite, it also helps him to find out exactly how late the woman is going to be.

In business, being late is less a form of impoliteness than a way of showing how special you are. If you do any business in French, when you first learn that the French for 'deadline' is *'délai'*, you laugh. The joke soon wears thin, though, when you realize that they're just being honest.

How late you are for a meeting is a measure of your importance. If you arrive on time, it probably means that you haven't just left a previous meeting, which suggests in turn that no one is interested in your opinions. Basically, get there *'à l'heure'* and you're a nobody.

I've sometimes found that your 'right to lateness' is in proportion to the size of the diary you lug around with you. People may even snub electronic diaries in favour of a huge appointment diary, the implication being that an electronic one is physically not big enough to contain all their appointments.

There are, of course, limits to lateness. In my experience of dealing with the French, a boss can get away with strolling into a meeting twenty minutes late, smiling and apologizing hypocritically for their *retard*. Lower ranks – the cattle of the meeting – should be there about five minutes late, preferably armed with a coffee so as to fill the time before the decision-maker arrives, and to make sure they get enough caffeine into their system to stay awake during the interminable discussions that are about to begin.[36]

However, if you have an appointment with anyone who holds your fate in their hands – a doctor, say, or a solicitor, bank manager, estate agent or absolutely anyone working for the state – be there on time. They can be late, because they're important, but if you dare to do the same you're implying that they're not important, and your fate is sealed.

Do the Write Thing

Letter-writing in French is another of those skills that makes you feel as though you've been transported back in time to the court of Louis XIV. Instead of neat sign-offs like 'Yours faithfully', the French use endings that can take as long to write as the letter itself.

The opening to a formal letter can be very simple you write just 'Monsieur' to a man and 'Madame' to a woman, or 'Madame, Monsieur', if you're not sure who'll be reading it – but your farewell takes for ever. Even if you

---

[36] For more on interminable French meetings, see the Second Commandment.

have met the recipient and named them at the beginning of the letter, you have to sign off with something like *'Veuillez agréer, Madame, l'expression de mes salutations distinguées'* – 'Please allow me to express my distinguished salutations' – or *'Je vous prie de croire, Madame, Monsieur, à l'assurance de mes sentiments respectueux'* – 'I ask you to believe in the guarantee of my respectful sentiments.'

You can almost see the writer bowing and scraping as they thank the recipient of the letter for deigning to give attention to their worthless cause. Presumably this is a hang-up from having to write to implacable administrative offices begging for your case to be heard, because the subliminal message seems to be that even if the recipient ignores your request or continues to screw up your life, they are still sure of your distinguished sentiments of guaranteed respect.

Thankfully, things are getting very slightly less formal, so if you've had a few dealings with someone – say an estate agent with whom you're sorting out a house purchase – you can end a letter *'Bien à vous'* or, even less formally, *'Cordialement'*.

In any case, these days, I'm pretty sure that no one actually reads those long formal endings any more. If you get really fed up with someone in an official position, you're probably safe writing *'Veuillez agréer, Monsieur, l'expression de mes détestations irrespectueuses.'* Probably.

What's in a Nom?

The French claim to have killed off their *aristos*, but it's just not true. The society mags are still full of pictures of unnaturally tanned people called the Baron de this and the Comtesse de that, all of whom will expect to be grovelled to.

The *de* prefix before a surname, suggesting a link to the nobility, still counts for a lot. Just look at the life of ex-president Giscard d'Estaing. His father, Edmond Giscard, a civil servant, bought the right to use the noble d'Estaing title in 1922, after claiming to be related to an admiral of the same name. More than eighty years later, as if to prove to the snobs that he was truly *classe*, Giscard himself bought the fifteenth-century Château d'Estaing in the Aveyron from the religious order that had been living there. He announced that he was going to use it in part as a family archive. No one could now claim that his family were not true d'Estaings. His life's work, the justification of a noble name, was complete. And they say the Brits are class-obsessed.

Don't be fooled by a double-barrelled name, though. In France, they're rarely chic unless they have at least three barrels. Two-part surnames are usually just a symptom of present-day political correctness, with married women keeping their own surname and tacking their husband's on the end. Coupled with the French love of double-barrelled first names, this can produce ridiculously long email addresses. In my old company, where emails were all on the model firstname.secondname@

company and there were lots of feminist women, the firm's email list was peppered with addresses like marie-bernadette.villepin-dechirac@multiword-company-name.fr. By the time you'd written half the address, you'd give up and phone instead.

Merde is Everywhere

When they're not being excessively polite, the French can be astonishingly obscene.

It can take a while to get used to the way that French swearwords crop up everywhere in the media, at all times of day, as if they weren't rude at all. Like women's breasts, swearwords are considered to be perfectly natural parts of human life.

I recently heard a French 'comedian' (I use quote marks because the term is often rather approximate) do a sketch on a mainstream breakfast-time radio show about how a politician had been looking more cheerful recently. Not because of an economic upturn or improved opinion-poll ratings, but because he had found a new girlfriend and enjoyed a *coup de bite*, a bit like saying he'd 'got his dick wet'. The image of a politician's private parts is not something I want to laugh at or even think about at any time of day, let alone over breakfast. (Now you see why I used the quote marks.) But on this show, his genitals were brandished about with complete disregard for decency and broadcasting standards.

The word *merde* hardly causes a stir anywhere, and

when doing interviews about my books on French TV and radio, I've only ever met one person who didn't want to say it. This was a radio interviewer whose show was also broadcast in Africa, and who was obliged, she said, to use 'correct' diplomatic language. 'It's OK for you to say it, though,' she told me, and I did.

Despite this non-shockability, French is still a great language to swear in. Not only because the words can be so descriptive (see the small selection below), but also because they seem to be chosen out of sheer relish for the sound they make. Rather than being spat out quickly like English swearwords, they can almost be sung, so an exchange of insults can turn into a kind of operetta.

Con ('bloody idiot', 'twat' or 'moron') has its regular feminine form, *conne*, but this can be made even more insulting by adding the *'asse'* sound, which the French find deliciously vulgar. *Connasse* (female idiot), and the even more pleasing *pétasse* (approximately: female farting idiot) are big favourites.

Other insults that can be elongated in the mouth and therefore enjoyed to the full include a male adaptation of *con* – *connard*, which allows the French person to prolong the vulgar-sounding growl at the end of the word – 'konn-AAAAARRR'.

Then there is *'enculé'* (often pronounced 'on-koo-LAAAAY'), a word that suggests you are an idiot because you have allowed yourself at some point in your life to be sodomized. Not everyone would take that as an insult, of course.

Porn to be Wild

The French are as open about porn as they are about using pornographic words. One of the five main terrestrial TV channels, Canal +, offers its subscribers hardcore porn after midnight. And the channel has only just introduced a parental key-in code and a completely blank screen before you key it in – until very recently, the porn was simply scrambled, which did little to hide what was going on during certain close-ups. Or so I'm told, anyway.

This porn is produced by French film-makers (although the actresses are often imports from the East, where girls will apparently do a lot more for less money), so the channel presumably gets grants from the government for showing home-grown culture rather than Anglo-Saxon sex. Before the film, the channel shows a 'news' programme in which they review new movies and show a 'making of', which is exactly like a porn film except that there is a man with a video camera in shot, and you see the girls wipe themselves with facial tissues at the end of a scene. Or so I'm told.

Softer porn, meanwhile, is everywhere. It is perfectly acceptable for a prime-time family film to show bare breasts, buttocks and people bouncing on beds. Janet Jackson's nipple would not have caused a ripple in France. Sophie Marceau did the same thing at the Cannes Film Festival, and no one in France suggested banning live TV broadcasts. Besides, the French see much more overt stuff on advertising billboards and news-stands. French porn magazines regularly do poster campaigns, so that a newsagent's window looks like an advertising campaign for sex. A pouting woman, who clearly can't wait to pull the photographer's trousers off with her teeth, points her breasts at passers-by of all ages, her splayed crotch hidden only by a headline like 'I Want More Sex'. Not that I've looked that closely myself.

Anyway, all this flesh and sexuality is on open display, to be admired by schoolkids as they pop in to buy their comics. Whether it's a healthy thing I don't know, but it's there, literally in your face, the whole time.

A List of Useful French Insults

(To see how to get the best out of saying con, you might like to read the short section on French pronunciation in the Fifth Commandment.)

Con ('ko' – with closed 'on' sound). Bloody (male) idiot, moron, twat, dickhead, etc. General insult aimed at a man.

Don't jump to hasty conclusions if you are called a *con* – it can be a term of affection. If you make a good joke or do something wacky, the French might say '*t'es con*', meaning you're daft, but in a good way. And in the south of France, conversations are peppered with *con* or *putain con* (literally, 'whore bloody idiot'), which aren't insulting at all – they're just embellishments, like 'd'you know what I mean'.

Conne ('kon'). Bloody (female) idiot, cow, etc. General insult aimed at woman. Note: *conne* is never used affectionately.

You can escalate *con* and *conne* by adding *gros* (pronounced 'grow') for a man, or *grosse* (pronounced 'gross') for a woman – meaning fat. France is still a fattist country.

Salaud ('sa-lo'). Bastard.

Salopard ('sa-lo-PAAARR'). A more fun way of saying bastard.

Salope ('sa-lop'). Bitch, female bastard.

To make these even more fun to say, the French some-

CONTINUED...

times string them out by saying *'espèce de salopard'* or *'espèce de salope'* (pronounced 'es-pess da . . .'). Literally this means 'sort of bastard/bitch'. It is up to the recipient of the insult to decide which sort they are and take offence accordingly.

Enfoiré ('o-fwa-ray'). Stupid bastard, dickhead (literally, an old word meaning covered in *merde*).

Tête de noeud ('tet danner'). Dickhead (an exact literal translation).

Tête de con ('tet dako'). Dickhead (literally, head that looks like female genitalia).

Va te faire enculer ('vat affair ong-koolay'). Fuck off, bugger off (literally, go and get yourself sodomized).

Va te faire voir ('vat affair vwar'). Get lost, fuck off (literally, go and get a seeing to). The French sometimes, and usually when joking, add *'chez les Grecs'* – by the Greeks – presumably a politically incorrect reference to that nation's alleged sexual habits in ancient times.

CONTINUED... ➡

A List of possible retorts to the above insults

Ta gueule ('tag-eul' or, more effectively, 'tag-EEEUUUL' – rhymes with 'girl'). Shut your gob.

Ta gueule, connard ('tag-eul konAAARRR'). Shut your gob, you dickhead.

Elle t'emmerde, ma gueule ('el tom-mayor-d, mag eul'). Literally, My mouth shits on you. Retort to '*ta gueule*'.

Casse-toi ('kass-twa'). Get out of here.

Dégage ('day-gaj'). Get out of here.

Pour qui il se prend, celui-là? ('porky eel s'pro s'lwee la') or, if it's a woman, **Pour qui elle se prend, celle-là?** ('porky el s'pro sell-lah'). Who does he/she think he/she is? Retort to *Casse-toi* or *Dégage*.

Finally, if you're fed up with the exchange of insults, it's best to turn away, sighing philosophically, and say: *Tu me fais chier* ('toom fay shee-ay'). You're boring me to death here (literally, you are making me shit).

As boredom – *ennui* – is the worst possible state to be in according to the French existentialist philosophers, this implies that you are setting yourself above this lowly exchange of insults. Even if what has really happened is that you've used up all your obscene vocabulary.

Some not-too-polite words for English speakers

Rosbif ('roz-beef'). English person (literally, roast beef. This is often used affectionately.)

Angliche ('ong-leesh'). English person (humorous French pronunciation of 'English'. Can also be used affectionately.)

Ricain ('ree-ka'). American (abbreviation of 'Américain').

Amerloque ('ammer-lock'). American (a condescending version of 'Américain').

Since the Iraq War and the coining of the word *'globalization'*, slang words for Americans have been used much less affectionately in some sections of French society. But see page 257 for the real French attitude to Americans.

French men are incorrigible romantics: 'My darling, missing you terribly, wish you were here at the conference, your loving husband.'

THE 11TH COMMANDMENT

Tu Diras 'Je T'aime'

THOU SHALT SAY 'I LOVE YOU'

THOU SHALT SAY 'I LOVE YOU'

FALLING IN LOVE WITH A FRENCH PERSON IS FRAUGHT WITH danger. I didn't realize this until it was too late and I was dumped for not saying 'je t'aime' often enough.

The French say it a lot. It pops out as often as a smoker's cigarette packet. It's as if they suddenly think, oh, I've got nothing to do, I know, I'll say 'je t'aime'. This is undeniably very pleasant when you're on the receiving end. You bring someone a cup of coffee and they say 'je t'aime'. You think, wow, what would have happened if I'd brought a biscuit as well?

But after a while it can be counterproductive. They've said it so often, and at such incongruous times, that you start to think, OK, I heard you the first time. Or worse, who are they trying to convince? Which is a terrible thing to think when someone is saying the magic A-word. But you can't economize with your own outbursts of 'je t'aime'. If you try to save them for special occasions, you're done for. As I learnt when I was dumped.

'You're not romantic enough,' she told me. 'You never say you love me.'

'I do,' I protested. 'I just say it less often than you. Like, less than once an hour.'

'You never send me flowers or call to say you've arranged a romantic evening and that the taxi's waiting outside.'

This had me stumped. For one thing, the only cut flowers I like are really big, blousy ones like tulips and sunflowers, which my *amoureuse* (or ex-*amoureuse*) found vulgar. And the whole 'taxi's outside' thing was a throw-back to her ex. He used to do that now and again and she loved it. I did arrange romantic evenings, but too often, it seemed, I actually consulted her on where she'd like to go. Democracy and equality, I thought. Cold English indifference, she decided.

'My ex was so romantic,' she said, the warm glow of blind nostalgia in her eyes.

'The one who was always cheating on you? The one who dumped you the day before your birthday? For a girl with a rich dad?' Oh, yes, he was romantic all right.

But it was no use objecting. She could only remember his non-stop bouquets and the veritable hurricane of *je t'aime*s that he'd whispered her way.

The thing is, like so much in French culture, love is about style rather than substance. There are florists all over the place in French towns, and French husbands rarely fail to pick up a few roses on their way home to their wives after a quick bout of adultery. And as his wife is putting the blooms in a vase, the husband will be text-ing his mistress to tell her he can still feel her luscious nipples pressed against his lips. Oh yes, French men are romantic all right.

Getting it on the French way

So what is the best way to succeed in the game *de l'amour*?

To answer this, it is vital to understand French mating rituals.

As in all countries where the two sexes are allowed to go to school together, French mating usually begins amongst classmates. There are almost no single-sex secondary schools, so French *lycées* are just as much like dating agencies or hormonal experimentation labs as the American high schools we've all seen in teen movies. What's more, the *lycée* is for fifteen- to eighteen-year-olds only, so there are no pre-pubescent children to giggle when more mature students feel like exchanging saliva in the corridor.

In one way, *lycées* are more healthily sexual than British schools, because no French schoolkid has to wear a uniform. This means that the French don't go in for gymslip fantasies. To a Frenchman, a girl in school uniform just looks like an air hostess for a low-cost Romanian airline.[37]

University can be a slightly tougher time for French kids to get together, because almost none of them leave the parental home to go and study in another town, so they don't experience the fun of having a room out of

....

[37] Though there is probably a niche market for Romanian air hostesses, too, as there is for all fantasies. A British friend of mine told me that he got rid of a French trainee after he found the young man looking at a website featuring naked old ladies chained to trees.

earshot of their parents. And, unlike Americans, few French students have cars to use as mobile bedrooms. The only consolation is that French universities are on strike so frequently that students will often be free to frolic during the daytime when their parents are at work.

Some Brits think that the lack of pubs in France must make it more difficult for people to meet each other, but there is really no need to worry on their account. There are plenty of clubs, bars and parties, and internet dating is the one thing about the web that the French have mastered. What's more, unlike in politically correct, hung-up America, men and women actually look at each other in the street, and let each other know that they're interested in what they're seeing. If eye contact and a smile are exchanged, French men are very adept at accosting a woman to tell her that she is beautiful and would be making the biggest mistake of her life if she didn't agree to come for a drink at the nearest café.

The workplace is also a popular place to meet a partner. Here, the French have a major advantage over some Anglo-Saxon countries. Sexual harassment is illegal, and a misplaced hand on a colleague's anatomy can lead to dismissal or prosecution, but a simple compliment will not be taken as a declaration of gender war.

This compliment cannot be along the lines of 'Oh, what spectacular breasts you have, Madame.'[38] I have been told some horror stories by French women who

. . . .

[38] Just for information, this would be expressed most effectively as *'Vous avez des seins remarquables, Madame.'*

appreciate sincere compliments but feel like thumping a man who oversteps the line. One woman friend of mine arrived at a meeting with two male colleagues to find that there were only two chairs in the room. 'It doesn't matter, you can sit on my lap,' one of the men said. 'No, thanks, I'd rather sit on the floor,' she replied. The French may be open about sex, but they do know the difference between chat-up lines and stupid sexism.

Workmates who want to find out whether they have more in common than a love of sales figures will probably start going out to lunch together, because French colleagues don't go in much for casual socializing after work, the traditional time when the Brits loosen up and swap shoptalk for sweet-talk.

After a couple of lunches, there will be the invitation to an early-evening drink or dinner, almost always coming from the man. The woman will usually wait to be asked out. If two people are getting on well and the man doesn't suggest taking things further pretty quickly, she will either assume he's not interested in her sexually, or that he's too much of a wimp for her to bother with. If the drink or dinner goes well, and the mood is relaxed, both parties know full well that the woman will be propositioned.

If the man says that he'd like to cook dinner for the woman at his place, and she accepts, then she has practically agreed to spend the night with him already. If she goes to his apartment and the man doesn't make a move before the last crumbs of his dessert have been sensually swallowed, then she will be mortally offended and probably refuse any future invitations on principle.

The French love to talk (and to listen to themselves talking), so the actual propositioning probably won't take the form of a lunge across the settee. At dinner or over a drink at a bar, the man will tell the woman that she is the rare orchid that he has been seeking all his life in the jungle of love. Or that an inexplicable emotion has been troubling him ever since he first set eyes on her – it is the feeling that his life will be like an eternal night if she is not there to bring sunlight into it. Or simply that he can no longer resist the temptation to kiss her. All this means, of course, is 'I'd love to have sex with you', but as long as the man obeys the conventions of poetry and politeness, the woman will welcome the offer. She won't sleep with him unless she wants to, of course, but she won't accuse him of being a sexual predator who takes advantage of women who accept innocent invitations to dinner. In France, there is no such thing as an innocent invitation to dinner.[39]

Homme Is Where the Heart Is

Anyone looking for a French partner has to understand the gender roles involved. And because France is such an

....

[39] On a purely practical note, a woman accepting a dinner invitation might find it useful to take a pack of contraceptives (*préservatifs*, pronounced 'pray serve a teef') along with her, because most French men are ignorant of their existence. And later on, she should not allow herself to be fooled by a Frenchman's claim to be suffering from 'condom allergy'.

old-fashioned country, ladies must naturally come first... [40] During the opening gambits of the game of *amour* (and, in theory at least, any subsequent relationship), the man must open doors for the woman, help her on with her coat, tell her she's beautiful – which is actually a very pleasant rapport to have. When I was at university in England in the early 1980s, I had a girlfriend who, if I held the door open for her, would ask whether I thought she was too weak to open it for herself. And if I told her she was beautiful, she'd ask why I didn't say she was intelligent. French women want equal rights in the workplace, but they enjoy old-school pampering from their *homme*. They're feminine as well as feminist.

French women also manage to be sexy without seeming at all tarty. They rarely show off their navel unless it is a perfectly sculpted navel. They can often be very sensual and provocative, but it's more of a ballet than a lapdance. Because of the formalized French seduction game, they don't need to get blind drunk and yell 'Wanna shag then or what?' in a man's ear.

French men are often confused, to say the least, by the forwardness of some (not all, of course) Anglo-Saxon women. An English friend of mine told me that she was kissing a Frenchman in a bar when she noticed that he was getting a bit too excited too soon.

'Oh no,' she told him, pushing the poor man away. 'I only wanted a snog.'

That's something that a French woman would never

....

[40] Sorry, but this is a deliberate double entendre.

say. If she's decided that she wants to kiss a man, she usually wants to do a lot more, too.

Being fundamentally macho, French men often try classic entrapment techniques. A favourite amongst arty Parisian men is the old 'come out to dinner and I'll tell you how I can help you get published/get a film role/work in TV, etc.' trick. French women pretend to fall for this, but usually go in with their eyes wide open. If the man is cute, they think, why not sleep with him? If he's not cute but he really can get them a job with a TV channel, why not sleep with him? *Les Françaises* know what they want and they know how to get it.

A woman who is looking for a relationship naturally hopes that the gallantry the man has shown before they slept together will continue afterwards. The problem with this theory is that one French word for sleeping with someone is *conclure*, to conclude. '*Tu as conclu?*' a Frenchman will ask his friend the day after a hot date – meaning 'Did you get what you wanted?' But if sleeping with someone is the conclusion, it doesn't bode well for life *après*. There is a scene in a film called *Gazon Maudit* ('Cursed Lawn'[41]) by French comedienne and director Josiane Balasko in which an adulterer and his mistress are sitting at a restaurant when a man comes in selling roses. 'No thanks,' the adulterer tells the flower-seller, 'we've already screwed.' French women smile rather wryly at this joke.

....

[41] This title has nothing to do with gardening, as it would if it were a British film. It is apparently a lesbian term for a woman's 'lawn'.

Some French men are considerate, good listeners, stylish, funny, and always available to take a woman out for a great evening. As in so many other countries, they are gay. Or they are straight and on their best behaviour because they haven't yet got the girl into bed.

The others fall into three basic groups. There is the smooth Latin Lover, the Anguished Artist and the Gérard Depardieu. All of whom are pretty macho in their own way.

The Latin Lover is, of course, testosterone on legs, a stylish seducer who will be forgiven for disappearing after the first night or cheating on his partner because it's in his genes.

The Anguished Artist exists on such a high plane that he can't do the washing-up. He will, however, be very good at borrowing the woman's money so that he can buy her lavish presents.

The Gérard Depardieu might give a woman a slap but he loves her really. (I'm talking about the roles Gérard plays, of course, and not the man himself. I am sure that Monsieur Depardieu has never raised a hand to a woman in his life, except to light her cigarette.)

The singer Serge Gainsbourg somehow seemed to combine all three models. And although he was ugly, often drunk, and presumably reeked of tobacco smoke, it worked brilliantly with women. He is even quoted as saying, 'If I had to choose between a last woman and a last cigarette, I'd choose the cigarette, because you can throw it away more easily.' French women didn't love him any less for it.

But – and this is a major *mais* – the Anglo-Saxon man

in search of a French partner does not have to adopt these tactics in order to succeed with French women. A*u contraire.*

French women love Hugh Grant. He (or his 1990s movie persona, anyway) is charming, sincere and washes behind his ears. On top of this, he is slightly naïve, unsure of his charms, almost unwilling to impose himself on a woman. The complete opposite of the Latin Lover, who does seem to get on French women's nerves now and again.

I did a radio interview once, a panel show about Englishmen and sex. The presenter suddenly remembered the Hugh Grant prostitute scandal, and began to say how shocking it was. And I quickly realized that what he found so shocking was not that an actor could be caught in his car with a hooker's face hovering over his flies, but that Hugh Grant actually had a willy. Yes, this archetypal Englishman was (gasp) capable of sex.

It's a reputation that is not without its advantages for a Brit abroad. A Parisian woman once told me that she was at a party, and a typical Anguished Artist type was coming on to her. He was telling her that she ought to come and spend the night at his place. No obligations, they could just look at the stars and talk about modern sculpture.

'Oh yeah,' she told him. 'You really think I'm that naïve? Forget it.'

'What if he'd been English?' I asked her.

She hesitated for a moment, then laughed. 'I probably would have believed him,' she said.

'Actually, there's a great view of Ursa Major from my apartment,' I mentioned casually.

Piquant Mix

A mixed Franco-Anglo relationship is a practically obligatory cultural-tourism experience for anyone living in France. What's more, if you play your cards right, hooking up with a local can solve all sorts of accommodation problems. What better way to find an apartment than to move in with your new *amour*?

But all cynicism and property-finding issues aside, the long-term mixed relationship has major advantages and disadvantages.

The biggest plus, I have always found, is that you can blame any gaffes on the language. 'No, chéri(e), you misunderstood me,' you can claim if your French other half erupts into tears or fury over some stupid thing you have said. You then have several minutes to backtrack and think how to say the exact contrary in mangled French or simple English. Similarly, if you are being ranted at in a foreign language, it is relatively easy to tune the ranting out and carry on reading your book or watching the football on TV.

These conflict-evasion devices are great tools for bringing harmony into an otherwise stormy relationship. And given the French love of talk and melodrama, Gallic partners can be very good at storminess.

The downside of a mixed relationship is that it can be

very high maintenance. Adapting to a new culture by speaking the language and driving on the required side of the road is one thing, but when this adaptation extends to the way you eat and drink, what makes you laugh and what you say and do in bed, the pressure can be hard to deal with. It is somewhat embarrassing when you are in bed and your partner is saying something apparently very urgent to you at a critical moment, and you have to ask for a translation or explanation. Please don't ask how I know.

Then there is the question of what you expect from a long-term relationship. An English friend of mine says that before she got married (to an Englishman), she lived by the mantra, 'French boyfriends yes, French husband no.' Her French boyfriends made the effort to say '*je t'aime*' and buy flowers, but they were just too traditional for her. Sure, they were happy for her to devote time to her career, but it would be nice if she did the cooking, too. And, she felt, if she'd had a child with a Frenchman, it would have felt as though she now had two kids to look after.

However, this theory does not take into account the fact that France has very generous maternity leave – and, in many companies, paternity leave – and that in urban areas, French childcare facilities are second to none. It's no coincidence that we use the French word *crèche* for our childcare centres. Paris municipal *crèches* often charge daily rates proportional to salary, and are open from eight in the morning to seven at night. Providing they get a place at the *crèche* – which isn't guaranteed – working mothers have no problems enjoying a fulfilling career, even if their husbands pretend not to know how to unfold the stroller.

Meanwhile, perhaps for exactly the same reasons, pretty well all the Anglo men I know in France are with French women and happy to be so. Sure, you have to remember your daily *je t'aime* quota and be willing to put up with existentialist debates on *Le Couple*, but the whole feminist-but-feminine thing is designed to make daily life feel pretty damn sexy.[42]

In any case, French men and women have absolutely nothing against mixed couples, and if the worst comes to the worst, they will accept splitting up as an opportunity for more melodrama and a rant against globalization, so you have nothing to lose.

Lover's All You Need

Foreigners with a French fiancé or fiancée are often surprised to discover that in France, it is perfectly legal to get married twice.

No, this has nothing to do with polygamy or bigamy. Well, not exactly.

If a couple wants a religious ceremony, then they have to have two weddings. The first one will be at the town hall, officiated over by the mayor or a town councillor. The second service will be in church. Because France is

---

[42] What's more, being French, there's a good chance she'll be a decent cook.

a secular country, a religious wedding alone is not legally binding.[43] Double-tying the knot doesn't guarantee a stronger marriage, though. Adultery is an institution in France, especially amongst the most respectable people of all, the Catholic bourgeoisie. The Catholic city of Lyon, watched over by a thousand statues of the Virgin Mary like so many stone CCTV cameras, is famous as a civilized hotbed of cuckoldry, with people living completely double lives. Husbands take time away from the office to meet their lovers, who themselves are the wives of the men doing the same in the hotel room next door. Secretaries send out bouquets to both lover and spouse, and never confuse the two. It is an institution, a system that no one disturbs by doing something so vulgar as getting jealous or threatening divorce (which is a mortal sin for Catholics, anyway).

None of this is flaunted, because that would spoil the polite social veneer. It is an unavowed law of nature, the equivalent of a bodily function that you don't impose on other people.

Politicians, too, are expected to have lovers. As Paul West says in A Year in the Merde, a politician without a lover is like a sheriff without a gun – people think he has no firepower.

....

[43] This law ruined a French film I once saw. The premise was that a poor West African man was posing as a priest to earn a living and get a roof over his head. He started doing weddings, which would have had wonderful comic possibilities in an Anglo-Saxon country, but fell totally flat in France, because the people he claimed to be marrying were all married anyway.

The conventional wisdom is that the French don't care about politicians' adultery. This is untrue. They love to read about sex. When President Chirac's extra-marital adventures were chronicled in a book by his chauffeur, the French were fascinated by his success with women (and his alleged speed when 'dealing' with them). President Mitterrand's love child Mazarine was hounded by the paparazzi, and is now something of a star in her own right. And when Nicolas Sarkozy's wife walked out on him with her lover, and Monsieur Sarkozy took his own lover on holiday to Mauritius, the French media went into a feeding frenzy.

However, the big difference is that the French don't judge. They love to read the exposés, but no one howls for the politicians' resignation, because the French don't see how it could stop them doing their job. On the contrary, a politician's job is to seduce the voters. So what if a few people are literally, physically seduced rather than just lied to on the election platform? A good adultery scandal will only boost a politician's ratings in the polls.[44]

If the French media don't disapprove on the public's behalf, this is not just out of respect for the law preventing the press from intruding into people's private lives. That would be relatively easy to get round by claiming that their reporting of the affair was in the public interest. It's also because journalists don't want any

. . . .

[44] Although I have never heard this said of a woman politician, so maybe the French aren't as open-minded about the subject as they think.

stones they cast to bounce back and hit them. What magazine editor, for example, is going to whip up a public scandal about a minister's indiscretions with a researcher, when he's been doing exactly the same thing with one of his reporters for years? And what upright bourgeois citizen is going to express disgust at the minister's misbehaviour, when he or she read the magazine article about it while lying in a hotel bed between bouts of illicit sex? The French can be hypocritical, but they're not stupid.

The politicians' wives, meanwhile, remain aloof or silent. Despite the revelations about Chirac's fondness for the ladies, Madame Chirac carried on as First Lady, apparently unperturbed (if the continued rigidity of her hairdo was anything to go by). Whether she was pleased at the revelations is another matter, of course. But at least in France she would never have to watch the interrogation of her husband on TV. No French politician would ever have to say, Clinton-style, 'I did not have sex with that woman.' After all, in Mitterrand's case, it would have been a pretty silly thing to say.

Playing (Away) with Words

Adultery is so ingrained in French culture that it has its own, rather charming, jargon.

An overnight bag is called a *baise-en-ville* or 'screw in town', the implication being that someone coming to the city on business is actually staying over for less professional reasons. The French have also formalized the concept of the *cinq à sept*, or quick sex session between five and seven o'clock after work. In the old days, when France had hundreds of brothels, this was the time when men went to visit prostitutes. Now it's usually used to refer to a less professional meeting. So while British office workers are at the pub having a post-work drink, the French may be enjoying an altogether different aperitif.

There is one essential set of phrases that prospective members of the *cinq à sept* community will need to know:

Une chambre avec un grand lit.	*Oon shom bravek uh gronlee.*	A room with a double bed.
Pas besoin de petit déjeuner.	*Pa b'zwun da p'tee day-djeunay.*	No need for breakfast.
Je peux payer en liquide?	*Dje peu payay o'lik-eed?*	Can I pay cash?

Let's talk about love, chéri(e)

Some useful phrases if you want to score points in the game of amour. First, some typical French chat-up lines.

Vous habitez chez vos parents?	*Voo zabeetay shay vo paro?*	Do you live with your parents?

(A French cliché as bad as 'Do you come here often?' It's basically a pretty direct way of asking whether a girl has to be home at night, or, even better, if she has an apartment where you can go.)

- -

Accepteriez-vous de boire un verre avec moi?	*Aksepteriay voo d' bwa runvair avek mwa?*	Would you agree to having a drink with me?

(A very formal, non-threatening way of asking someone you see in the street to have a drink at the nearest café.)

- -

Qu'est-ce que vous faites dans la vie?	*Kess k'voo fett donla vee?*	What do you do in life?

(Notice that they don't say 'for a living'. This is to allow aspiring artists who might actually be bureaucrats to say 'I write' or 'I paint'.)

- -

Quel est ton signe astrologique?	*Kel ay to seenya asstrolodjeek?*	What star sign are you?

(As in other countries, a favourite cliché amongst men who want to show that they have a sensitive side. If you are asked the question, to avoid having to learn the French word for your sign, in reply simply sigh: 'Amour'.)

CONTINUED...

C'est drôle que le destin ait fait croiser nos chemins.	*Say drolk l'dess-tan ay fay crwuzay no sh'ma.*	It's funny that destiny caused our paths to cross.

(*A clever way of suggesting that it is written in the stars that you are destined to have sex together.*)

. . . .

Tu as les yeux les plus expressifs que j'aie jamais vus.	*Too ah lay zyeu lay plooz expresseef ka dja djamay voo.*	You have the most expressive eyes I have ever seen.

(*If the person you are trying to chat up is wearing sunglasses, just exchange 'les yeux' for 'la bouche' – mouth.*)

Some phrases that might be useful if things get heavier...

Tu es l'orchidée rare que je cherche depuis toujours dans la jungle de l'amour.	*Too ay lorkiday rah ke dje share sha deupwee too-djaw doh la djang-la de lamoor.*	You are the rare orchid that I have been searching for all my life in the jungle of lurv.

. . . .

Je ne peux plus résister à la tentation de vous embrasser.	*Dje ne p'ploo rayzi stay alla tontassao o d'vooz ombrassay.*	I can no longer resist the temptation to kiss you.

(*If this seems a bit hard to pronounce, a simpler version would be...*)

CONTINUED...➤

| Je voudrais t'embrasser. | Dje voodray tombrassay. | I would like to kiss you. |

(*A couple may still be calling each other* vous, *in which case the phrase would be 'Je voudrais vous embrasser'. If this is the case, the kiss can help to make the transition from* vous *to* tu. *Of course, there is no absolute need to say anything before kissing, but the French love conversation, so this remark could be regarded as a sort of pre-kiss foreplay.*)

- -

| Chez toi ou chez moi? | Shay twa oo shay mwa? | Your place or mine? |

(*If your place isn't convenient and the other person doesn't have one of their own, it is acceptable to follow on with . . .*)

- -

| On va à l'hôtel? | Ova allotel? | Shall we go to a hotel? |

And when the relationship has begun, the use of key phrases becomes even more essential...

| Je t'ai apporté un cadeau. | Dje tay aportay uh kado. | I brought you a present. |

(*A useful phrase, as it can cover everything from flowers or chocolates to a new watch or a pet goldfish. An essential phrase, too, that must be used regularly to maintain a harmonious relationship with a French person.*)

- -

| Non, chéri(e), tu m'as mal compris. | No, shayree, tooma mal kompree. | No, darling, you misunderstood me. |

(*To be used instantly if your non-French attitudes provoke any kind of tantrum in your partner.*)

CONTINUED...

Je t'aime.   D**je tem**.   I lurv you.

(The ultimate essential phrase. Like ultra-mild shampoo, it can be used as often as possible. It is also the nuclear option if your tantrum-control methods break down. Even at the very beginning of a relationship, it is highly unwise to say 'I think I love you'. You do or you don't. It is an absolute, like being alive or dead.)

. . . .

Moi aussi.   *Mwa oh-see.*   Me too.

(This must be said instantly in reply to every 'je t'aime' if you want to avoid being accused of not loving the other person.)

. . . .

Tu m'aimes?   *Too mem?*   Do you love me?

(To be said with a worried look if the other person has not said 'je t'aime' for the past five minutes.)

. . . .

Bien sûr, chéri(e).   *Bee-ah syoor share-ee.*   Of course, darling.

(To be said instantly in reply to the previous question.)

. . . .

Non, tu ne m'aimes pas.   *No too na mem pah.*   No, you don't love me.

(To be said instantly if the other person does not reply instantly 'bien sûr, chéri(e)'.)

. . . .

Mais si, chéri(e). Ce soir je me suis dit que nous pourrions aller dîner à ...   *May see chare-ee. Seu swarr dje ma swee dee ka noo poor-eeo zallay deenay ah ...*   Of course I do, darling. I was thinking that we could go and have dinner this evening at ...

(...and quickly insert the name of an expensive restaurant. This will be taken as conclusive proof that you do love the other person. NB: don't forget to cancel the date with your lover.)

Epilogue
THE LOVE THAT DARE NOT
SPEAK ITS NAME

THERE IS ONE TYPE OF LOVE THAT IS RARELY, IF EVER, mentioned in polite French society. No, not homosexuality, which is fairly well accepted. The Mayor of Paris is openly gay and people don't care at all. With his annual *Paris Plage* – the artificial beach along the banks of the Seine in summer – he has added a certain gay exuberance to the city's staid cultural life.

No, the love that dare not speak its name is the unavowed adoration of the Anglo-Saxon.

As I've said in previous chapters, the French will spit upon the concept of fast food, but gobble hamburgers. They will turn their noses up at Hollywood 'trash' and flock to see *Star Wars* and *Spiderman*. They will wax lyrical about Dior fashions and dress themselves head to foot in Nike. They will lament the fact that English is killing off all the world's other languages and be first in line to sign up for English lessons when their employer asks who wants to work in the international division.

A grumpy waiter might pretend not to understand English, but in most cases he will feel good about his ability to speak the language, and not only because he can rip the naïve foreigners off for a few extra euros. To speak English is to be hip and modern.

And let's face it, the same is true for us Anglos. We laugh at the French, but we love them really. They are arrogant, but we wish we had that much self-confidence. They're old-fashioned, but we'd love to be that stylish. They're hypocritical, but we envy their ability to get away with it every time.

This is why all young French people want to go and live in London or New York, where they will be able to live this hipness for themselves, and get a job as a shop assistant without first having to spend three years at the *Ecole Nationale de Shop Assistants*.

And all Anglos dream of buying a house in France and living the French lifestyle, devoting their whole existence to food, wine, sex and dangerous driving.

But let's not spoil the game of seduction by coming out and saying this. For the last thousand years or so we've both been playing hard to get, and by and large, apart from the wars, one burnt French saint and a few port blockades, it's been fun. If we give up the game now and declare our undying love, we're heading for disaster – a quick, probably unsatisfying, afternoon at a hotel, post-coital blues, and smoking in bed.

So let's keep our love for each other secret. It would be a shame to spoil things after all these years, *n'est-ce pas*?

Index